RAGEING

Rageing

JOE R MEYER

Dedicated to Delia, Mikaylah, Dad, Jennifer and David who inspire me to think, ponder life, your life, my life, love, loss, success and failures. Without this thought I am but a shell of man who would feel nothing, God forbid. Thank you for all your acceptance and my weirdness, my constant need to write, to express and be me. These thoughts were created with love and great strain to my growth as a person, something I work towards each day and night.

Contents

Introduction

Blogging continues to bring my soul comfort in the mist of adversity each day. Although like any person I have my moments, which blogging has allowed me to express my true self, without judgment, pouring out my heart onto the white canvas each week for others to read. For those who don't blog or read blogs they are truly missing out of the freedom one experiences allowing me to be vulnerable in a world that is often filled with division.

This is third volume, which goes more into depth, and I can say this is this the largest volume thus far, where my voice continues to be strengthened in my values and beliefs in my continuous openness. My blogs continue to be a source of inspiration and expression for my family to read, especially those times when we can't sit down and have deep conversations. Writing allows me to speak and share with the world but specifically with my wife who reads my blogs, as she has a better understanding of who I have become over the years.

The readers of my blogs may not really care about my life, but many do, often getting comments and messages, which confirms to me I am reaching some. I can understand I am not everyone's cup of tea, especially when I write about the dystopia that has become the United States in which I live. What I have seen about these volumes is the number of pieces I wrote and alarm I shared with, what is happening in our country and the changes we are experiencing. I have used my blogging as a form of record keeping, history accounting if you will for this point in time, as this volume written between 2024/2025 and a lot has certainly happened, especially being under the threat of dictatorship and King Trump. There I go along going political, not a side to me I enjoy writing about, as I would prefer to write about more positive subjects such as love, peace, my faith, family, but unfortunately the tide of this volume is considered very political.

One thing that is certain about this volume that I discovered is although I spoke about my faith, I didn't write about it as much as previous volumes, which leads me to believe my mind and state of mind have been more in a state of fear. When I am in this state of fear, my anxiety and my depression create unrest in my heart and my mental state diminishes and today's political climate has only made it worse for me alone. What has also impacted this volume is my financial turmoil in both 2024 and 2025 affected me severely, I am surprised I survived. There are many pieces I wrote about my mental state in these years, especially my severe suicide ideation, but writing is my refuge to my thoughts and of course my family. I am sorry to say I can not help that death is a common theme in my writing and pray one day my readers will see a change in my thinking, but the pain I experience in my life can be intense.

One of reasons I continue to create these blog books is not just for historical records for my family, especially my daughter Mikaylah. But I write for the world to have a record of my existence, although my existence in this world has no real meaning as I am a nobody as opposed to a world leader, political leader, public figure who the world puts on a pedestal. These blogs will hopefully be around in infamy for my daughter and family to read in case I cease to exist anymore.

There I go anything speaking of inevitable demise, but deep down I pray for time with my family, years of writing my blogs, books to leave something that has my voice. This blog is apart of my voice and I own it.

Part 1 – Mental Health

Content note: This book discusses depression and suicidal thoughts. If you or someone you know is in immediate danger, call your local emergency number. In the U.S., you can call or text **988** for the Suicide & Crisis Lifeline.

Chapter 1

Why Do We Try So Hard to Prevent Suicide

January 15, 2024

Hear me out because often especially in the U.S. we make great efforts to prevent suicide. The know the answer may be oblivious such as "Well because their life matters" or "they need to live" . But why do they need to live, who are they living for , for family and friends who will soon forget them. Friends and family who make no real efforts to build meaningful relationships. Death is apart of life, why must one suffer, struggle going to life unhappy, searching for things that may never come to fruition.

I often think why am I hear, as I have live a life of struggle, of being mistreated, misunderstood, pushing forward for a good life only to be told no, while I look around seeing people in great prosperity with a great career, money, security, love, friendship, good health and seemingly not a care in the world. Yes I know you may say everyone has something to worry about, everyone goes through shit.

So, does Elon Musk, the richest man in the world struggle, does he fight life traveling on his private jet or does Jeff Bezos of Amazon struggle on his Yacht. Does the president of the United States struggle with anything but old age being in control of free world.

Yes there is pain in the world, pain for those who just want to pay their rent, have a good job, food to feed themselves and families which seems impossible today , so why not just end the suffering, be done and done, no one struggling, suffering or worrying, sounds great. So why do we try to take this gift from people when you are not going to pay their bills , feed their families or them, give them a steady job , the bare necessities of life. Why do you care if others die especially your family and friends, let them.

Often even the people we strive to provide for, protect are ungrateful. Often you hear kids today say I Would NEVER take care of my parents, NOT my responsibility, to each their own, screw them. In those many cases why not just end it, family doesn't appear to care and only need you for your enjoyment and benefit. Why not have a MASS suicide day so people can be out of their misery, to make those friends and family happy.

Again why do we in our society try so damn hard to save people who don't want saving and don't need it but prefer to be left alone to die on their terms.

I am not advocating to go off yourself, but keep an open mind.

I personally plan my own demise one day to finish what I started back in 2007. But don't worry not today as I have planning to do before i leave this world, because yes I have a wife and daughter I want to leave financially secure because why should my choice devastate them when if financially secure the can go about living , survive and thrive without me and live far better lives without me in it. As I said in time I too would be forgotten but my family would still be here living their best life. I see too often people live better now that their loved ones are no longer here. I do worry about my spirit, will I go to heaven or hell of be earth bound to roam the earth as a ghost.

I don't why I had this random thought but had to get it out, I guess because I often think about my last days as much as I'd love to live a long, healthy life, prosperous life I don't think I can or will but will not leave my family without something to push forward.

I would say to fully prepare I need between 5-6 years of planning and to see if there are major events in my life to prevent me from following through like incredible wealth, big promotions at work or something miraculous that only GOD can create, until then I'll wait and see. I don't know one to end things today like so many do without proper planning leaving loved ones in worst states before one's demise.

For me it's a Mondays ! But it's also someone's last breath at their own hand. They are Free from a life of struggles and pain.

Chapter 2

Would You Die Voluntarily?

January 17, 2024

People often say I would die for you, whether it's their child, spouse , loved ones but how true is that. If you were the main provider for your family and were about to be homeless and had to die to save them that hardship, would you. Many would say NO , if we are homeless we will be homeless together as a family. But what if your life was worth a considerable amount of money which if you died they would get like life insurance, what you self sacrifice yourself so they could live, survive, have food and a home.

Again many would say I would NEVER do that, that's a ridiculous question. I get it because most would never end one's life voluntarily so your loved ones wouldn't suffer, but I would.

If my wife and daughter were on the brink of ruin and about to be homeless, I would sacrifice myself. If my daughter wanted to go to college and I had no money, I would do it. I would do it because in my mind their lives are so much more important than mines.

That's what I often think of when it comes to my family and NEVER failing them. Up to this point IVE failed them. Yes we have a roof,food, clothes and the necessities but I've failed them in providing them a better quality of life and in the next coming years I hope to change that but feel I may not. That is why I protect myself with life insurance, because frankly I'm worth more dead than alive and in my mind the would be able to live better lives without me.

I know we all like to say money doesn't matter , but that's a lie. Money matters, living a good quality of life matters, being poor is a sad , depressing and meaningless life at times as you miss out on the beauty of life that costs money.

I not say one necessarily have to be a billionaire but a low millionaire is nice. That is what I hope for my family, if I self sacrifice myself one day , they'd be set for a long time to live a truly better quality of life. Yes I know I'm not there but in time I'd be forgotten which I am used to being last. I'm used to not be thought of as this has been most of my life.

I know for most of we want to live to our last natural breath but what purpose, normally it's for others when we as people struggle, suffer and many say that's life, who wants to live this way, I don't. I want my family to prosper, thrive even if I'm not there and actually I'd be happy dying knowing they'd be ok.

So again would you died voluntarily? For your family and loved ones if it meant they'd have a better life then you could give them.

Lastly we live a money hungry world. Money makes the world go round which is not changing it's only getting worse as if you no money you are nothing in this life, I choose to have my loved ones be someone in this world even if we live in a broken world.

Rant over!

Chapter 3

Unhinged Again...But I Will Be Ok

January 20, 2024

This week I was having a real moment for some reason as my mind was filled with turmoil , thoughts of un-satisfaction. Thoughts of feeling as my life has no meaning as I self-reflected on my life which I do a lot as my heart struggles. I look at the mistakes of my life, the choices I made growing up especially in my twenties that I feel were lost due to me being in a deep depression, attempting to end it at only twenty eight years old.

Where Did I Go Wrong?

I think about where I went wrong and I look at my younger co-workers so are in their late twenties in the same position I hold and ask myself, how is it I could not have a position like this at that age.

How is it that they are living their best life at that age I couldn't yet filled with sadness, not wanting to live. At the time in my life I may have appeared happy, but anything but, but I really tried. I went to work each day, went to school , attempted to push forward but it meant nothing to me, it was a chore, something I had to do.

Times are a Changing for the Worse!

I think about my daughter who is only eleven years old and how I would NEVER want her to experience times like I have. That is why I make great efforts to be here for her, to love her, to talk to her and give her everything she needs and at times wants. I am kind to her, never attempt to give her a harsh word, even in my feedback I am kind or at least I try to be.

I don't want her to grow up feeling worthless like I have, but to know she has value, she is important. She is so much like me at times, which makes me proud but also scares me because I don't want her to have feelings like I do. I know it may have a lot to do with my upbringing of living with a so called grandfather whom I refer to as the Devil.

He would torment me each day, putting me down from the age of five, tell me how stupid I am, how I'd never amount to anything. A man who only cared for himself as I was forced into doing chores and using me as child labor on the weekends, never having the same childhood to go out and be a kid and nothing changed when I got older especially when I could drive as I was forced to take him places, errands and because I lived in his house I was RE-

QUIRED, could not say NO or I would get his attitude, his possessive person came out, his anger. He would be this way towards my mother and sister who also lived in HIS house.

Yes he would remind us each day we lived in HIS house, nothing was ours, we were visitors not to touch his things and if we did we would pay. Mom was required to cook and clean for him each day and me and my sister were his human slaves. Eventually my sister came of age and left , mom stayed behind and eventually I was told to leave. At times thinking why my mother stayed, angering me, why would she allow us to take that abuse over my young until adulthood. She died in his house on December 9, 2015 living a life of torment, sadness which I believe is what truly killed her although she was ALWAYS ill growing up, having some mysterious illness doctors were unable to diagnose. Dying of cirrhosis of the liver and no she NEVER drank. She lived of other sickness, its too hard to remember, but I loved her. She is in Heaven nothing giving her life to the LORD JESUS, Praise God I will see her one day.

Society Only Gets Worse!

I look around at this world of self-indulgence, of money, of wealth and of a message telling me how worthless I am because I don't have a large home, a mansion at that like this countries gods of the Kardashian's who throw in our face each day how much we don't have, as their life is stoved in our faces each and every day on our news feed, on television everywhere.

They are not the only ones of course, there are the celebrities that live the life of glitz and glamour, with their fortunes as they are permanent vacations while the rest of the suckers go to work each day, work 9 to 5's , making it barely. Then don't get me started on these countries GODs of Elon Musk, Bezos, Trump and others who rule is country.

YES I know GOD, Lord JESUS is in control and this world is in his control, but in the good Ole U.S. Those are the men and women who control our Televisions, on news feeds who do everything in their power to control us in society, so we are under their thumb. We allow so much garbage in our minds and news feed each day it makes me sick. We also have politicians, who act as mini gods who create laws to serve them and them alone, not the common folk, the peasants of society.

There is a lot of noise in the U.S. and to add to that the world is crumpling right before our eyes and I truly believe the U.S. is on the verge of full authoritarian government if Trump becomes our president, doing reversible damage we may never recover from. You see although the U.S. likes to present itself as be a world leader we are anything put. I get we are considered the greatest country in the world but believe we are failing our society as society is filled with greed, ruthlessness, hate, anger and corruption that only seems to be getting worse. Many of us are slim pickings to be taken advantage of by our government, society, nothing is the same.

Maybe it is a sign of the times, Jesus is coming soon as our world crumbles which is supposed to happen, Jesus proclaimed it but that doesn't mean it's a good thing right now in the sense our world is getting world and yes looking forward to Jesus coming back. But in the meantime, people are struggling, suffering and rely to much on man. Man, to save us, Man to fix our problems, as you have seen Men and women are expecting our future president to make the world a better place, but remember they are men and women, they are NOT god, they do not see all like GOD, they are not omniscient.

1984 is HERE!

But believe or our the U.S. is looking to look more like George Orwell's 1984 and many will scoff at that thinking that would never happen. I can happen because again men and women are weak, men and women only care for themselves and many are unwilling to stand up for what is right. We are in the age when even life will imitate art like in film, thinking of the films the Purge for some reason where our government would allow the thinning of society for 24 hours.

These are the thoughts the run through my mind each day, but its much more than what I am writing as my mind spins and spins and spins, which is why I need to write it out like I am a ragging lunatic. I have no hate in me, but I am angry, depressed, anxiety ridden ready to throw in the towel thinking that my love ones would be better off without me, at least they would have peace not to worry about me.

I want to have peace in my life and yes I need to have more faith in Jesus as he is the prince of peace. I lack faith at times, but Jesus has not steered me wrong, even in times when I screw things up, he fixes my messes. He fixed my 2023 and have fixed previous years, but I need to have more faith, no let this life bring be down although I have great responsibility, great financial responsibilities that when I think of them, would be so much better if I was just not here anymore dealing with those things.

Each day I try to start a new, being positive that life will be ok, but even I do not believe that at times as society becomes more destructive, dangerous where one can not just live life in peace but always worried about when someone will come and try to take our lives, take what we have. The thief is not who you think it is, it's not the thug, it's the people we work for, the people we give our money to each day, its corporate America.

I think a big part of these my thoughts come from is my observations of this world and what I watch at times. I am not a lazy person but like drama, supernatural, mystery as I have seen the X-Files, who hasn't, Supernatural which I am watching Now, SVU, Law and Order, Organized Crime and the list goes on. I get its only television and its plain old fiction but again art imitates life.

As you can see my mind is spinning again, I am raging again but hope I am making sense as I know many may feel like I do.

Continue to keep me in your thoughts and prayers!

Chapter 4

The Weight of My Life's Choices

February 4, 2024

I often reflect on my life, my choices, and where I am today in my life. I'll admit that career-wise I thought I would be much further into this life today. Although I am not complaining about my current state and the company I work for, I thank GOD. God has position me in a company that will allow me to learn new skills, expand on my current career and position strengthening my background in project management.

I Had My Time!

But I remember a conversation me and my wife had about my career, my life and in a way the dissatisfaction I have experienced. I remember my wife telling me "You Had Your Time" and she did not say it in a bad way. Only that yes is right when I was younger, like in my twenties

I had my time to enjoy life, have better life experiences, meet new people but I failed to do that.

The reason I failed to do that was because of the depressive state I was in during those years, which basically stopped me from living my life. Like many of you who have read my blogs, I struggled greatly in my life even today, struggling to gain my footing in this life, although I appeared to have all the tools to be ok, such as an education both a bachelor's and master's degree.

I am NOTHING

But for most of my childhood I was told I was nothing, worthless and wouldn't amount to anything. Hearing this from the age of five into my adulthood, it was a belief I was nothing but still went to school with the hope of bettering my life, getting gainful employment and being successful. My generation of Xer's were fed this hook, line and sinker about the importance of college and how if we didn't go, we would only work minimum waged jobs and not amount to anything.

Yes, I "Had my Time" and that time is gone and although yes I can build, rebuild, reinvent myself each day and nothing is over until its over once said by the great Rocky Balboa. I look around today, especially see the newer generations who seem far happier in this life. I know looks can be deceiving, its quite possible they are suffering, but choosing to live their best life differently, which I admire. My daughter who is an Alpha Generation or Generation A. There is an uphill battle for these generations which many of the kids of who are my age and younger and some older.

Life's Regrets

I feel great regret in my life and although I love my family, I can only think of how I am failing them now and each day. On the outside, yes, we have a roof, food, clothes, and transportation and what is needed for our day to day, but nothing more. I guess what I have is much more than what others have today and many are far worse off and struggling.

What I believe to be a big part of why I feel so insufficient is how much the media throws into our faces, how much we don't have , how our lives a meaningless compared to those that we are bombarded with, such as celebrities. But I understand that the celebrity themselves is not always the problem, it's the media who makes money off their image about their incredible life, compound that on social media times a million.

A Culture of Misdirection

We live in a culture of misdirection as we draw our attention to things that have no meaning. Many would say just ignore the noise, keep strolling, don't let those celebrities' lives get to you. I get it, I do as those celebrities mean nothing to me, but they do have an effect over our lives and the lives of many who attempt to mimic their lives, but in the end, I believe we live in a sad, sad world of depression, anxiety ridden society who are broken.

This Nation is Broken

I believe we live in a broken nation and world and its only getting worse. I attempt to make the best of it, live my life each day, go to work, spend time with my family and try to enjoy this life the best I can. The day will come when I need to make a choice, an irreversible choice to make sure my daughter and wife will be ok financially even if I am not there. My philosophy is their lives are worth much more than mine. There happiness is much more worth it then mine and If that means my wife and daughter can make it in this crooked world with money, then I am all for that.

Glutton For Punishment

Why is that people want to be glutton for punishment, to struggle each day until they take their last natural breath? What is the point of that. When I think of my daughter attempting to navigate her life when she gets older and have struggles finding work, surviving and it was me or her, I choose her. Some of you may think what the hell am I talking about.

I am saying in not so many words I am worth more dead than alive, but I would need to be dead for my family to benefit, which I am not quite ready yet, because deep down I still have hope and truthfully would not want to leave my eleven year old not have her father right now, but maybe when she is older like twenty, it would be less difficult for her because she would older and be able to survive on her own.

"I had my chance" and my wife is right because I made bad choices in my life, I was asleep at the wheel in my twenties, which affected my thirties and today. I can always remake myself, get a new job, new career, make more money and get all the things one thinks they need to be happy. I refuse to live a life where my wife and daughter will continue my curse of struggles in this life to survive, because I want them to thrive in this life, much better than I have and had and willing to do anything I need to make that happen within reason.

My Life Philosophy

My life philosophy may not mesh well with most because most look forward to living their lives to the fullest, never thinking about a final way out like I do. Lastly I know where my soul is going, whether I am here naturally or not, meaning if I die natural or by my own hand, although I would prefer to live a long natural life, but only if my family can prosper, can thrive in this life and I know it takes times and work, but how much time must I wait until I see true financial and life prosperity, because I have not seen it for years when I look around and see others have it , living their best lives while I struggle, suffer each day, how is that life. These are the weights I hang onto each day, have hung on to for years, years of regret fill my body, my mind and spirit, I am DONE.

Chapter 5

Epic Failures of Life

February 19, 2024

Getting older is no fun, although many would say that's life and that is so true as we have no control over age, getting older, only what we do with our time here on earth. In my older age I have become increasingly observant of myself, the new generations of today and although I am not old, only 44, I still can't help to look at others who I work side by side with, super successful people who are eons younger than me and, in my eyes, far more successful and who have done more in their short life.

I know we all have different walks of life, backgrounds, education, family dynamics that make up each of us, but I have FAILED. I should be a far better place in this life than I am today, and this is an area on contention I can not help letting go of. Do I attempt self-improvement, absolutely.

Am I well educated yes with both a bachelor's degree and master's in business administration and certifications. Do I have over twenty years of experience in the workforce, yes, but it has been a long hard road to get to where I am today. I am not saying people do not struggle to get somewhere, but it seems as though many reaches earlier success in career and life.

Constant Comparisons Today

I know we shouldn't compare ourselves to others, especially those much younger than us, but it's hard not to see that people seem far more successful in this life with less now.

I think at my younger co-workers who do the same job I am doing, making decent pay at such a young age, when I was their age, I feel I made peanuts. One could say well that's your fault no one's else's, you have a choice of what you wanted to be in this life, maybe those people are better are choosing better career paths.

I know people are right, I choose career paths, I thought would lead to success, to better opportunities only to get the shaft as the employer reneged, laid me off or fired me, causing me to restart again, again and again. I am not getting any younger, actually time seems to be speeding up where I get to a point that I am no longer considered useful in this life, ill admit that many get here.

I Followed The Rules!

I ask myself did I follow the rules like so many in our generation was taught, get an education, as much education as possible and doors will open, your incomes will great compare to just a high school diploma. Sure, spend years and thousands of dollars getting degrees that most employers do not even require. It just happens I liked college, but still wanted to have degrees and pay for something that would have paid off and it hasn't often worked in places with no degree requirements and no extra pay for having degrees.

I am led to believe and trust that it's also the college I went to, DeVry and Keller Graduate School of management. Nothing inherently wrong with those schools, only that many employers considered those colleges as a form of joke.

Yes there were years when I truly searched and searched, job hopped in search of what I thought I wanted from a career, realizing late that I should have stayed put at a certain job until I figured things out but I didn't do that, often changing jobs after a few short weeks and months, but that was when I was in my twenties no thinking that those years catch up to you. I see now that many who are successful at my age had a plan, stuck with a plan for building knowledge, experience and wealth and I didn't do that, so I failed in my career.

I know we all have a restart, we can all have second chances to rebuild, enter new jobs and careers and its as if history was erased which is what I have been slowly doing but again I am not twenties, I am in my forties and the new generations appear to be far more intelligent, quicker than me.

I do worry in how I am seen now in this corporate culture, am I seen as an old fogie, ancient, outdated, a Boomer or am I seen as an equal. I have found that at my age I truly need to prove myself continuously to show I am worried to be in the ranks with the younger generations like Z's and Millennials and eventually I will be seen like our older generations as out of touch but hope that doesn't happen for many years. In our society we tend to discard older people especially the elderly but believe they have so much to offer we often overlook them, writing them off.

That is one of reasons I write so that one day my thoughts will be remembered, my voice and words can be read to see that I did have a voice because there may be a day where I may be stricken with disease or lose my mind due to dementia or Alzheimer's which runs in my family.

Sadly, each day I see myself worse off as someone of value here and ask myself the question who I am, how did I get here and where I went wrong. These thoughts are regarding my career, not personal life although there are failures there too but today it's about my career failures.

What is The Point

Some may wonder what the point of this post is, was it just to complain and NO. It's meant to bring awareness of the value of time and how we need to choose how we use our time wisely each day especially when we are younger, because eventually time catches up with us and I can live in regret for those choices which will affect times in your time when building over the years pays off, especially when having families , bills and other cost of living in this life.

Today is me having a case of the Mondays, What else!

Chapter 6

The Spiraling of My Mind, asking it to Stop

March 13, 2024

I often feel inundated with information overload, doom strolling as my mind attempts to process the news of the day, the celebrities, the photos, the stories, and periodicals I come across every day.

Media only makes it worse

I should just turn it off, ignore the noise posted online, but my brain, my interest is to always be learning and be in the know, which is not always a good thing. For most, who cares what happens in another state, what happens to celebrities and what happens in the world of politics.

What I have seen this does to me is severely affect my mental health, depresses me as I only see articles on the elections, Biden, Trump, Senators, Republican's, democrats, Taylor Swift, Cardi B, Kardashians, Being rich, getting rich, Making money and basically how my life means nothing compared to the life of an influencer who make millions living their life around the globe.

Many would say, those images are not real, fake news and then add to that I go to LinkedIn, where I see mass layoffs, people on the brink of ruin, on the brink of homelessness, out of money, can't feed their families, out of work for long periods of time.

Doom Strolling and I can't stop

Ultimate doom strolling, why can't I stopped, as if I am looking for something, looking for something each day to stay positive, motivated with a focus on people like you and me who are just trying to be ok instead of the world telling us how worthless we are as humans. How we will NEVER amount to Taylor Swift and her 1.1 billion dollars, fame and fortune with her perfect life, No I will never live like her.

I will never be an Elon Musk or Jeff Bezos with their unlimited resources. Yes, I get these are all materialistic things, in GODS eyes they have no value. The rich have always existed in a sense even in biblical times as Kind Solamon was the richest person in the world at the time, probably worth more than Elon and Jeff Bezos in his time.

Hate Social Media

I know I sound like an old duddy fuddy, but I HATE social media, I have the fact that everything is at our fingertips at times and I know that sounds crazy, because for most of us we LOVE our devices, keeping constantly connected, but I do not need to be connected to the world, I do not need to know everything, I prefer to live in ignorance. I missed the days when I picked up a newspaper and read the news, limited my view on what happened in my circle and not have to deal with the million of different voices and opinions.

My brain hurts now, but then I have my current environment as I spend my days in the office as I look around and get to work with some incredible people. These people I find to be far more superior than me, smarter, harder working, more intelligent, more successful, no screws up like me as many of co-workers are younger than me and have higher positions, managers and leads making me realizing how much of my life I had professionally wasted and where I could be today if I am not let Depression get in the way of my life.

Why I'm such a screw up

Why have I screwed up my professional life in pursuit of being successful as I have always had good intentions for the companies, I worked with to work hard in hopes of moving up, but NEVER did it happen, NEVER did the employer see my value, but I stupidly hope even today.

I have always had this stupid hope of a brighter days, future where one day I can have peace in my heart and mind, but I do not as I feel a war continues inside of me each day. My mind races to all my failures and regrets in my professional and personal life as I failed as a husband, father, brother, son, as I remind myself each of that.

I am exhausted literally at times, each day when I go to work and try to focus. My mind is going to be the death of me one day as I feel my mind deteriorates further into the depth of despair, where writing gives me some relief into this madness as I expose my thoughts to the world as I live through the imaginary worlds of my books as I escape through my stories and try to live in other realities not my own.

I wish to be understood

I wish others understood me more as many will say to seek help, see a therapist, get on meds, do something. But I have found writing and daily exercise helps, but as I work in the office now 4 days a week and work nights 4 days a week, what time and energy do I have to exercise, where I can go a 4 in the morning or 10 at night, not ideal times, especially when I wake up at 5:20 daily. I am thankful I can go on Friday, Saturday and Sunday giving me some relief.

I need to do better in managing my mind, my stress levels, trying to stay healthy but its not easy as I look at myself and added pounds over last year curtailing my loss of pounds that have creeped back, depressing me further having almost two years of a healthy weight but not I feel like I am spiraling now as I cant help to equate my weight to my self-worth, thinking of myself less worthy.

The world of politics rage me

At times I am filled with rage over the world of politics, rage had the people who this country puts into power, true American Idiots which goes for both Dems and the GOP who spread hate, conspiracies, far fetch ideas to help the people who mostly sit in their ivory towers , many multi-millionaires who have no idea what it means to struggle, you scrimp by for every penny, what do they truly know about the working class, Nada.

Then we have future presidents, who are both ancient and though they still have their facilities, they are losing their facilities quickly with age. One looks always confused and other looks to be the next dictator of America.

One appears to have deplorable policies that will hurt or kill many people if elected and the other seems to want to help people both coming with huge price tags pushing our debts higher as one day we may fall into fiscal insolvency, Bankrupted America, how does that sound, that is where we are headed.

My wheels are spinning now and I need to stop, but thank you for enjoy this short raging ride with me, Have a good day!

Chapter 7

My Struggling Mind Each and Every Day

May 10, 2024

I often think about those who struggle with their mental health daily, those who work so hard each day to just keep it together, and how many are just on the verge of throwing in the towel. I don't think many feel the way we do about our lives. I believe that most experience the blues, bouts of sadness and depression but nothing that stops them in their tracks like many of those who struggle.

The Thought of Death

For myself, I think about death almost daily, about my way out and some may think, well you must have a pretty horrible life and I will say NO. I have a wife and daughter, work for a great company, also teach college part-time, but what gets me is all the responsibilities in this life especially in California, where I typically don't have much at the end of each month, sometimes nothing left.

Nothing to Show

My viewpoint is I have been working for over twenty years and I have nothing to show for it, I have not moved up in the way that I thought I would have. When I look at others who are especially younger than me far more successful in their careers, I can help to feel envious, feel as a failure in this life and failure as a provider, father and husband, which leads me to the path to what is the point of living.

Society Thrives as I Fail

I also look to society as it appears many are getting rich, living their best life, showing me my true insignificance I truly do believe and have for many years that people are just better without and although I hope that one day I will think differently, that one day I will say I am wrong.

I have failed too much in this life, I have had too many setbacks and I get life is not fair, not perfect, that we live in a broken world, a broken country and state. One would think by even bothering to keep up with what the world wants. I feel conflicted at times because I am a believer in GOD, in Lord Jesus and my thinking goes against what the bible says, because I am a weak man, I am broken.

I'm okay with Death

Sadly, I smile at the thought of ending my life one day, not for the fact that I am leaving behind my family, but in hopes of leaving them a better life of less worry about me, more freedom to live their lives and more money, a completely fresh start of someone who just brings people down.

This is where it may get a little stranger with my thinking as I think when I complete the job of passing on, I think about the afterlife. Now as a Christian and a believer I would go to Heaven and yes, I understand there is debate that I would not go to Heaven, but straight to hell because what I did was a sin, which is taking my life, but I believe when we give our lives to Jesus and we commit this act, God does take out salvation back.

My Soul Has a Home

I do not fear death as death is a natural part of life and I get many may say, well that may be true but I wanted to live a long life into my older age, so I could one day see my children grow up, have grandchildren, experience those incredible life moments and I agree I too would love to see that, but what is point of living like that poor, destitute without an ability to thrive in ones life of having what is needed to be okay. I get it we as people want to live,

I think about the homeless, many who live dismal existence on the street and frankly I do not understand why one would wish to live like that. I understand no one wants to be homeless, but how can someone who is homeless still wish to live. Maybe those who are homeless gave up on trying to keep up with this life and said they are perfectly content being free on the streets, living in the elements with no money, little food, or shelter and being susceptible to drug use and violence.

Better Off

I think if I was too die, would me dying before my time cause my spirit to stay here on earth, until some point in time I could move on, I think greatly about that as there is a spiritual world that exists. I think if my spirit was to stay behind, would I be able to see my wife and daughter and make contact with them and be apart of another world that exist beyond our own, I find that interesting and worth the ticket of dying.

I know many will say well don't you wish to see your daughter grow up and be there for your wife, what kind of many wants to just leave them by dying. Again I believe the loss of me will eventually surpass and they will move on to live their lives which is what I expect them to do yes I know it wil be hard at times, but in time it will get easier.

No Plans for Now

Now don't worry I am not planning anything today or tomorrow, more like five to ten years from now and there are certain factors that could change this outlook such as if things get better financially for myself and family, if my career moves in better directions.

One thing is for sure, my writing will hopefully live on as in my books, which once I am gone wish for my daughter and family to have control over the rights so they can do something with it so I can become the next Toiken turning my books into movies and television, making my family a large fortune to live a much better existence, you see to me it's about the quality of life they live, not my own.

It is hardbreaking that the suicide rate in our country (U.S.) has risen as the statistics are about 800,000 since 2000, with the higher percentage being Male. Could all of these be mental health related, its hard to say and I believe many think because one ends their life it could be because of mental health, but it could be economic, financial, family-related and a variety.

I remember a story of an elementary school principal by the name of Christopher Christensen who leaped off the Disneyland parking garage in December 2022. The man had been arrested due to arguing with his then fiancé or spouse, as she claimed he hit her, but he did. He was arrested and then released, then his employer put him on leave why they investigated the claims. I suspect he lost hope in getting his position back at 51 years of age and the stress was too much, jumping and dying instantly.

What is True Happiness

I get money doesn't buy happiness, but it sure does help. Would I even think of ending my life, if I had a million in the bank or $500,000 probably not, but when you have very little, or you live paycheck to paycheck, these things haunt me. Also please spare me , well you need to learn to save, you need to cut down your costs, like what, like Rent, like food, like basics. Oh and for those who say well move somewhere cheaper, not in California unless I live in the sticks of some part of California no on wants to live, nah and moving out the state is not a financial option, trust me I have heard it all and thought of it.

I don't expect, most to agree with me or understand my thinking, as many have said I should talk to a therapist and I say for what, so they can tell me my thinking is wrong. Are they going to be pay my rent, buy my food, make sure my family is okay...No I didn't think so. I am not saying therapy is worthless, but often times it's a trick of the mind, to believe and to at times disillusion ones self from the reality of how I am living right now. I am working towards getting better, but when will my relief come, when will I have peace as I have not had peace for years and I am tired.

I appreciate those who listen and may not agree, but you listen to my rants and my struggling mind and soul, hopefully none of you know the feeling, but if you do, then maybe you do what I do is hope tomorrow is better, but it could be worse and although I am not advocating to go jump off a bridge, just make sure you are confident in where your soul is going, heaven or hell makes a huge difference.

Lastly remember there are many who walk among you like myself, that one day may be there last day, so be kind to your fellow human.

Chapter 8

My Burnt Light

May 29, 2024

Have you ever felt like you lost your light in life. Do you ever wonder is this it, is this the happiest I will feel. Or Do you feel that your light in life has burned out. I think about this a lot as I think of a time in my life when my light for life was at the brightest.

Remembering My Light

Some of those special times included when I got married, meet my future wife, the birth of my daughter, raising her which is ongoing. Although I love my wife and daughter, the internal light for myself I feel is gone.

I tussle with these feelings because people will try to justify these feelings that that is normal to not feel the same all the time. But although I will continue give, love my family when it comes to myself, I have no more burn for life I once had as if my optimum has died. Although not an audible voice, the voice in my head fights these feelings, wearing my spirit and brain down even further as I fight myself on how I can recover my former self.

I Live For my Family

I have sacrifice greatly for my family, which I know is what it takes to raise a family, but often I feel I get nothing in return. That is not to say my wife and daughter give me nothing in life, of course they do, but I feel I give and give but in return I am unable to care for myself as I got to work, work two jobs, make barely enough to get us through the month at times, as war within rages.

I have found that I no longer live, but within my mind and my writing as I project my fears, hopes and happiness in my stories through my characters as I find at least with my characters I have control over their destiny.

I Live Through my Writing

My writing is what I hope lives on after I am no longer here, as maybe my writing it add some significance to my life as maybe my work will carry on like so many incredible writers. I don't think my writing will be world famous, but anything is possible as you look at Edgar Allan Poe, as his wring lives on centuries. I am in no comparing myself to Poe, but at least when you look at Poe's life when he lived, he too didn't appear to live a great existence and even a long life, dying quite young if I remember correctly.

I have learned to well to just get through in life, like zombie at times, go to work, eat, sleep, go to work, eat, ship, crap, go to sleep and then go to work. Like many of us, we may not realize we just go through life , forgetting to enjoy our days, enjoy the people but most importantly enjoy ourselves as people, then you get to point you don't recognize who you are anymore, you don't like who you've become and then worst case, your see how broken you are, which leads many to just end life, because they see their full potential is gone.

We rely so much on others like employers, family, friends to who us our value. As a believer in Jesus, he sees our value in us and yes he tells us we are valuable but at times we don't believe. Its not that we don't believe him and his words, its hard to believe God loves us so much yet as humans we fail to believe at times. There are those who do believe and I envy those who believe their true value.

I have yet to trust my value in this life, as I see there is life and death, we all will have die one day, some sooner than others although we have this notion that life is meant to last a long time, but maybe we should think about what our impact is at the time we live on earth. Some die so young, their impact may not seem to have made a difference but they.

Those Gone are Free

I often search obituaries and see what people write for people who had passed on and I looked their pictures and they ages at time, as some die young as babies, children, teens and my age and older. It's sad looking at these times, eventhough I don't know anyone I imagine what their life was like and find surprisingly many more women seem to pass than men.

Some of these women's pictures have them smiling, full of time, thinking they probably didn't want to die, wanted to live. I honestly wish to die I always hope my mind will change, that something miraculous will take place in my life where I say I want to live a long life, but in the end I see others are much better off without me as I am just a drag on everyone around me.

These are the thoughts that crowd my mind each and every day as I go to work, spend time with my family, pay my many, many, many bills.

That's Life!

Chapter 9

September is National Suicide Prevention Month

September 4, 2024

September is National Suicide Prevention Month and it's especially important for those who have lost friends or loved ones to suicide.

This month opens the discussion to those who are struggling, a discussion, a conversation that may change someone's life. One should look at the warning sides of suicide.

No one person is alike and one who things of suicide doesn't necessarily mean they are mentally ill, it could be they are struggling with challenges they are unable to control or fix like financial matter, health matters and other personal matters.

For Most the thought of suicide doesn't cross their mind, because most want to live, but there are those who struggle, who think about it, but there are signs such as:

1. Talking about wanting to die wanting to kill oneself
2. Talking about feeling empty, hopeless or having no reason to live
3. Talking about feeling trapped or that has no solutions
4. Feeling unbearable emotional or physical pain.
5. Talking about being a burden to other
6. Withdrawing from Family and friends
7. Giving away important possessions
8. Saying goodbye to family and friends
9. Putting affairs in order, such as making a will or arranging home and financial logistics
10. Taking great risks that could lead to death, such as driving extremely fast or using drugs and alcohol more often
11. Displaying extreme mood swings
12. Planning or looking for ways to acquire lethal weapons, stockpiling pills or purchasing a gun.
13. Showing rage or talking about seeking revenge.

Sadly, many of these above are what I experience and honestly, I never used to be like this. I have always struggled with mental health concerns going back to high school as lived in a verbally abusive home. As I grew old, I managed, but depression never goes away.

Today I experience these symptoms because I have had great uncertainty for myself and my family, such as Job losses, financial challenges and being able to properly support my family.

Yes, we have a roof over our head, food on the table, but that's a challenge. Its difficult for me as I watch the parade go by as I watch others have great success in their careers, families and have the simple things I want for my family like a family vacation but cant.

I know my struggles are not uncommon, but for me its so much more magnified as these are personal failures that look me in the face each day as I plan my exit strategy all along thinking my family is just better off without me, at least with out me they could have a more financial support and have a sense of peace in their life. I get it they won't have peace at first with me gone, or my other family.

The hard truth is no matter how often friends, family and colleagues tell me how important I , how valuable I am, I don't see it. It's not that I think they are lying to me, but I don't believe because frankly I look at myself each day and I see no one special.

I believe that's where the main struggle is that you can tell someone you care about them and love them, but if we don't believe it then what's the point. Many do suffer in silence, cry at night, during the day and stay silent because most don't want to burden people with our heavily load and from my experience many just don't want to hear it, they just walk about, even unwilling to listen, so I gave up even trying.

Its difficult speaking to my wife about how I feel and she knows, and assures me we will be okay, but at the end of the day, I can only think of how little I offer her life and how she deserves so much better then a broken man, and daughter who deserves a father who can give her the life she deserves. In my eyes its all about what the deserve, which is the best and I have failed to provide that despite me working hard.

Lastly there is an incredible stigma against speaking about mental health that one is labeling unstable, crazy, nuts, so many different words and shunned for be honest. e

Thank you for all those who listen, keep me in your thoughts and prayers! I try to live day by day, but its difficult when I think about the future of my family and where they will be as if I attempt to see the future,

Chapter 10

Finding Gratitude Amidst Challenges

November 25, 2024

Happy thanksgiving!

It's difficult to be thankful at times, but we must. I have a difficult time do this at times, although I have a lot to be thankful for like a Job, two in fact. I am in good health overall, but my mental health continues to take a toll on me. I have a my wife Delia and daughter Mikaylah who are healthy as well.

This time last year, was difficult as I was still fairly new in my job, having had a terrible year in the job market and I was at that point my worst possible point in mental health.

This year was better than, but still not as great as I struggled financially to recover from last year, but the scars are still there and today. Sadly, I cannot shake this feeling and its hard to force myself to be thankful.

I am gravely conflicted as I look to the words from 1 Thessalonians 5:16-18, Rejoice always, Pray continually, give thanks in all circumstances for this is GOD's will for you in Christ Jesus.

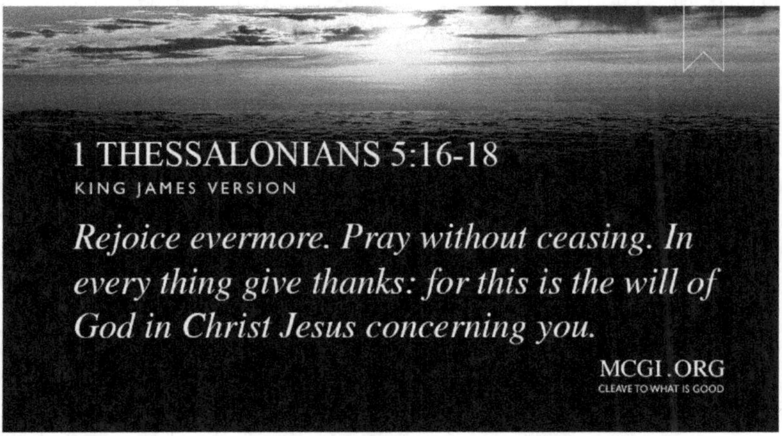

I ask myself, how I can be thankful each day when I feel my life and my family's life teeter totters in the balance financially as I am the holder of the purse and have done what I can to do my best, but have failed at times, even today. The thought of self-destruction continues to haunt me each day, as I search a way out and to give my family what they deserve a father and husband who is deserving of them, I am not him.

I know that people go through far worse things than I do, and they are still thankful and all I can say is its supernatural in their thankfulness, because frankly how could people have Joy during times like major illnesses, thinking of children who are suffering with horrible sickness like Cancer as I think of those St. Jude commercials.

During these times, I feel really affect many as they look around and try to self-reflect on what they are thankful for and all I can say is there are a lot stronger people then me out there in the world, so what see my troubles as trivial.

One can say being thankful is a choice, I need to choose to be thankful and think of the good in my life today, look to JESUS and how he wants me to be. I pray GOD fills me with the spirit of thanksgiving this season to know what is important in this life and not focus on those things that don't matter. When I look around I see the country and world in turmoil and it hurts me to see this, although Jesus warned us all, but its difficult to see it come to fruition especially when I have a daughter who is only 11 growing up in this world and its only gotten more nasty and I ask how can I be thankful for that. Yes it's a sign the end of times is coming, and although I am not prophet, no nothing of what the end will look like Jesus knows, but it could days, weeks and years, maybe even decades and centuries before Jesus comes back and claims Us.

One thing is for sure about this day is the history of its existence between some of the first pilgrims and indigenous people who at first formed an alliance for military reasons and then over time learned from each other. I love how Abraham Lincoln in 1863 made his Thanksgiving proclamation giving birth to the holiday.

Thankfulness has and is apart of our country and culture today and I am sure many Christians like me practice thanksgiving as preachers preach on the importance of it. I agree its important, but some one like me can be difficult, as my mind tends to think only of what I don't have to be okay.

At the end of the day, I am thankful for my wife, daughter, Sister, father, brother-in-law, heck even the pets in my life of the people in my life.

God bless all of you during this week and season

Chapter 11

Giving Myself the Gift of 4 more years of Life

December 11, 2024

The holidays are a time of self-reflection. What we consider to be most important. Although one could look at life and see and say I have nothing to be down about and in my opinion, there is always something we could be down about, life is not perfect after all. For myself I have my wife and daughter whom I love, but I cant help to think how much better their life would be if they had more.

As the main provider I struggle to give them the things they deserve, although we have a roof over our head, food on the table and the ability to functional and have a relatively normal life, but financially I am a mess. Over the last ten years I have failed them miserably. When other families within ten years have prospered financially, we have not on account of my lays off , instability of the high cost of living, food and rent, having a good car, which often requires purchasing every ten years, as I work to make the car last. At the same time trying to provide things to my family slightly better then we had before like a better car and apartment. We are not fancy expensive vacations, frankly we don't go anywhere as a family and haven't been for some time due to money.

Heartfelt Marriage and discussions

My wife and I often have heartfelt conversations about the finances, as I see how hard she works at McDonald's. The amount of abuse she takes from her co-workers, who treat her like a second class citizen, like a person undeserving of dignity and respect. One would say why doesn't she just go elsewhere, and believe me she has tried and has gone to other employers as they treat her almost the same way.

God bless my wives heart for her dedication to be a good employee, respectful, always willing to offer a helping hand, providing kindness to those around her. But often she is mistreated, disrespected, told to be quiet. She often works with younger employees in the age range of 18-35, who treat her like shit and this is coming her managers as well.

In my heart she works so much harder then me, putting her body on the line physically, while yes I sit in an office and a virtual classroom, rather simple jobs for me, but I see each day how her work damages her body and although she is still young, the effects of her work will one day take effect on her body, as she has seen women who have worked for McDonald's decades as they grow older, they bodies are affected. It pains me to see that she has to do this job as I think why cant I make enough for the both of us, so she doesn't have to work and I know that sounds old fashioned, but I see that as failure on my part, a poor provider for myself and my family.

Worry and Anxiety a Constant Nuisance

My wife and I are constantly in sync to worry and anxiety of the finances as I am on the brink of Bankruptcy once again, everything under my name of course, a name and credit tarnished, but that's okay, rather me than her. But she still worries for me constantly and in a way she should, as I am losing hope each day, pushing forward to the new day, new month and years to keep providing, but each day I have grown weaker and giving up.

I know we shouldn't compare ourselves to others and what others have, we are by no means trying to keep up with the joneses, just trying to survive, save money, have prosperity like many others do. Again, I know I shouldn't compare, but I look around with others who have prospered greatly with homes, money and alike giving their families the peace of mind. I know it takes work and time and I do try, but something always seems to have happen right when things are going well.

This year has been difficult and it continuation from last year and the job loss, but in his case, the finances ballooned out of control as I attempted to adjust my new salary along with the changes in my wives work schedule which is not always consistent as the manager cuts hours freely which affects us financially.

I attempt to move on from last year and what took place with the job loss in March 2023, getting a job in May and then unfortunately losing the job again in July and then getting this role I am in now in September, those huge changes in income have affects that don't just correct themselves once one get s a job, there is a build up of trying to survive as I had to relay on credit to make sure we were okay , had food and a roof over our head. Yes I made mistakes relaying on those things to be okay, but it was that or we would no ability to get food or pay rent, then what homelessness, not on my watch.

My Experience is Not Unusual

I know that many out have experienced similar out of work situations often more devastating then my joblessness, where many have been out of work for six months, a year, two years, something I would not have the ability to recover from. At this point, I don't think I can recover in what is happening financially unless I file BK soon and it that is not approved then I will need take matters in my own hands and cash in the life insurance policy for my family. I know it seems pretty drastic and most would not take that route, but I am sadly comfortable take that route if it means my family will be okay even if I am no longer around.

Assuming once I can file my BK, it will be four years of evaluation for me as I give myself 4 more years of life to prepare my family for my departure. You see no matter what I still have the plan to end my life, which I know is heart breaking to hear, because why would I do that if we are okay financially. Because deep down, I see myself as a failure to my wife and daughter and that will not change, they deserve better. My hope is that will end my life, because who wants to die , its so messy and traumatic. I believe things can turn around for me, I can have peace once again in my life, and have security once again.

My Festering Angerand Depression

Over the years, anger has festered in my heart, disappointment, sadness, depression and a slew of emotions I battle with each day. Being a people observer, when I go to places like mall or shopping center , I cant help but to look at the body language of others, and although I don't know those people, you feel a sense of peace in their life like everything is okay, something I wish I had.

I am aware that those same people may be struggling with far worse things like financial and health battles. I know my wife wants to truly see me be the person I once was when we first met, so full of life, happiness and yes

I know marriage and responsibilities change a person in different ways, but not always in a bad way. Marriage although difficult, should make a person better and don't get me wrong my wife has made me better, but she has also made me realize my weakness as a man, father, husband and provider and even though she never says anything, I know myself how I have failed her.

I can't help to think about love and happiness, and I understand one truly does not know if another person is happy. I would like to believe that most are happy and content with their life, although life is not perfect and will continue to search for that peace. I actuality I should be at peace in my life no matter what, being a follower of JESUS as he tells us not worry, do not fret, a command that is difficult, but not impossible.

Looking For The Signs of My impending Departure

I will continue to look for the signs as there will be milestones as I evaluate the next few years, but anything could change, as I could easily make a drastic decision to end my life tomorrow, which would severely affect my wife and daughter, not just financially but in other areas like work and school, something I really don't want to do. I do have a hope of one day being promoted, which would in a way make up for me being here. I also have so many stories to write, to blog and Vlog about before I depart leaving something for my daughter.

Some reading this may think that I things I find important are really not that important after all like money, but money makes the world go round and without that, nothing can truly be accomplished. I am not asking to be a millionaire or billionaire, but that would be nice, I would settle for have a few extra grand as a nest egg and my belief continues to stand that I am worth more dead than alive.

I struggle at times as I conflicted over this view and my Christian faith, but understand I am not alone as I have reflected here times that there have been men and women of faith to take their lives, which goes to show you that the human side is weak. As much as we want to say just stick it out, push forward, everything will be ok, but in reality, it may not be so again I ask am I just to live and suffer in silence.

My silencing

It angers me when I attempt to speak up about it , I am often told to be quiet, don't talk like that instead of someone saying it will be ok, don't feel that way. But often I am told to go seek therapy, get on meds, but that will NOT do anything, tried and done that as I have struggled with this for over twenty years. Death is apart of life and people are forced to recover as people lose friends and loved ones each day, life goes on.

My heart is at war right now as GOD says Joseph, I am here, I will get you through this, depend on me and I say "LORD, give me peace, give me strength, help me another day". I am not heartless to want to leave my family behind but in my mind, I continue to see I have no worth in this world and maybe that is the problem too, I compare the value my life to what society says is valuable.

Only GOD knows the future, only he knows , what the next five years will look like, but I know its up to me to try to have a good state of mind, not let things get to me and go with the flow, but that is hard at times when now I see what I have lost this year trying to get it back. Getting a glimpse is something that I will carry with me any years but will try.

I understand that many struggle with insecurities, being without, some without food, shelter , some in poor health and yet they push forward, I do not know if that is me or not, because I wait for my last days. I am hopeful too that my state of mind will change, that I will want to live and I do.

Each year I will evaluate until year five and it's possible at that time, Life and I will be at a place where I feel no need to end it, I hope.

The added stress is what is going to happen in our country in the next four years, which some may say that has nothing to do with my feelings, but it does as our country is unraveling into instability and uncertainty to what the job market and economy will look like. Yes I am working right now, but hopefully that doesn't change. I will continue to try to stay positive and look forward to each day, but at this point I do not.

Chapter 12

The Hidden Struggles of the Holiday Season

Original title: The Hidden Struggles of the Holiday Season: A Call for Kindness

December 20, 2024

During this time of year, the holidays. I often think about the amount of grief and sadness people are going through. I believe that this is time when suicides are at the highest levels as many go through this time of year feeling lonely as they look around who appear to be happy, have happy lives.

I tend to go through this today, as I begrudgingly go to the mall or the store for Christmas shopping I look at the people, their faces, their body language, how they spend, what they buy. Looking at their faces I see happiness, sadness, frustration, worry. I wonder what some of these individuals go through, if they will be alive in future years.

During this time of year, people are spending, giving and going to debt, some more then others, put themselves in financial harm. Now I get that many spend this time of year because frankly this is this the time when people tend to spend making up for the year. In the United States we are full of consumerism, spend, spend, spend and then in January we feel the effects. Now some may prepare for this time of year, but many cannot.

Many will attempt to get past this month, many have not been able to and have called it quits, finding that there is no reason to tis the season to be Merry, even if watching all the Christmas classics may help but usually wont. One of films I find great solace in is Charles Dickens A Christmas Carol. Having watched the films, story a true reminder of how the human spirit struggles and how there have been no shortness of people who go without as Crachit and Scrooge display that perfectly. Another film that displays the importance of life especially during the holidays is Its Wonderful Life.

Although I have been provided for in my childhood and into my adulthood, I know what It means to want and need, although not to the extreme of others who are homeless and without food.

Money doesn't buy happiness which is true, but it does give you options to get help like seek therapy, get proper medication and eat and live better, this all helps.

Recently there have been some very public suicides in the media, one specifically is Stephen Boss, Ellen DeGeneres DJ died by suicide on December 13th, 2022.

A man I had no knowledge of prior to his death but that is simply because I do not watch Ellen and or follow the dance world. This man appeared to have money, fame, a family who loved him and was in film and Television. Just today saw an article that Cmdr. Robert Ramirez III, 47 died by suicide, who was decorated navy seal commander.

Lastly recently in a nearby town of Anaheim, California, a suicide at the Disneyland parking structure by the name of Christopher Christensen.

These are just a couple examples but per the CDC are is 1 death per 11 minutes due to suicide. Here is where this information is from : Suicide Data and Statistics | Suicide | CDC. This number is astounding and very sad.

I personally know what it means to have attempted many years ago, I obliviously did not succeed, it just so happens my sister came home at that exact moment, saying she was feeling ill. I was hospitalized for about two weeks after my 72 hour hold was done. I believe these feelings of depression developed over childhood, a childhood filled with verbal abuse from my grandfather, divorced parents and being overweight and bullied. Over years my self esteem stay low, feeling I could and would never amount to anything .

After graduating college I was lost, had no direction of where I wanted my life to go and received no guidance from family and friends, I really was alone although I lived at home seeking help. Over the course of my life since 02/ 07/07, I have gotten married , had a child, live and work, pay bills like anyone else.

I still struggle with depression at times, question my self-worth in my job and just my life. I know I am loved and not contemplating anything so no worries. But for those struggling with negative thoughts, thoughts of suicide, one should speak with someone, you are not alone.

This is where the story takes a turn, I often ask myself why is Suicide stigmatized in the media and by people. I get that we are taking our lives, a life I believe doesn't truly belong to us but GOD. A life we had not choice in but God gave us life and we are taking it. As a follower of Jesus, I struggle with this, because I truly believe GOD does not want us to suffer, but in a way he does.

Frankly the people who truly love those who die and complete this act are their family and friends. In the end we all die. In the end time passes by , years go by and eventually that loved one you lost is almost forgotten, but people move on with their lives.

Should people live in agony and one's agony may be nothing to most of us but something for someone else, like finding love. Its amazing how many people are searching for a loving companion, a boyfriend/Girlfriend, even a future husband and wife spending years searching. I know that was me, because honestly I just wanted someone to spend time with me, love me and accept me for who I was, but many years ago I found no one, just rejection.

There are those who suffer to get somewhere in life career wise and don't get where they wish to go, eventually it becomes too much. Others have unrealistic ideas about money and wealth , feeling their life amounts to nothing without those zero's in their bank account.

Thinking of those people, we look at those who have everything we want, money, wealth, fame, attractiveness , a so to speak beautiful life, but often items in the end those who have that don't appreciate and value what they truly have. Often you will find those who have nothing sometimes literally the happiest. We all have and want things that make us personally happy in this life.

One the relationship I have today that has kept me going is GOD, more specifically Jesus. But sadly I have seen today is Pastors who should have the strongest relationship with Jesus die by suicide, like Jarrid Wilson a Harvest Church Pastor who also led a minister on mental health.

In addition a lead pastor by the name of Andrew Stoecklien. No man or women is immune to depression, to anxiety to committing such acts, its all tragic.

Know life is not perfect, most will not live a life of a celebrity, life of a millionaire and billionaire, remember there are around 8 billion people on this earth. 8 Billion souls who are searching for meaning, the meaning lies with those in our life like family and friends. You may say well I don't have any friends or family, I am alone. You are never truly alone, GOD is there, he has not forgotten you, he loves you. You may say well I am not really a church person, I don't believe in the politics of church, the hypocrisy of those followers. The truth is most if not all of people are hypocrites, no man or women is perfect. Despite the look of a persons perfection, they are not perfect, Only GOD is perfect.

During this time of year, if you are feeling down and out, worthless, remember you are not, you have value even if people are not around to tell you. But if you decide to take the dreadful act of suicide , I just want to say I am sorry your soul is so sad, that humanity has failed you in showing you kindness and love.

If you do decide to take this act, please let others know why, especially those you live behind, don't leave leaving loved ones in despair blaming themselves. Those who are left behind may truly not know why, if they are to blame or if you suffered in silence which you shouldn't.

I get we live in a rotten world and its only getting worse especially if you look at the politics of our countries today, the greed, the hate and hypocrisy but at the end of the day our government, our jobs, our co-workers could care less about our wellbeing, they have no skin in the game of our lives, but our mothers, fathers, brothers and sisters, sons and daughters, they have real skin on our lives, the ones who love us, who love you.

We truly don't know what others struggle with, be kind, be generous to those around us. We are all just trying to get by this life. Give yourself a break and know that everything it will be ok, not perfect, but you have control to do things in your life.

Don't allow those around you to bring you down, bring down your spirit but know you are unique and special with your own set of talents and gifts unlike anyone else.

Lastly if you are having thoughts of suicide and self-harm please speak with someone, in the U.S. you can dial 988 and or 911 for emergency.

Have a blessed and safe new year, Don't drink and drive, call a ride share if you are going out. May you have a blessed 2025.

Part II – Social Justice

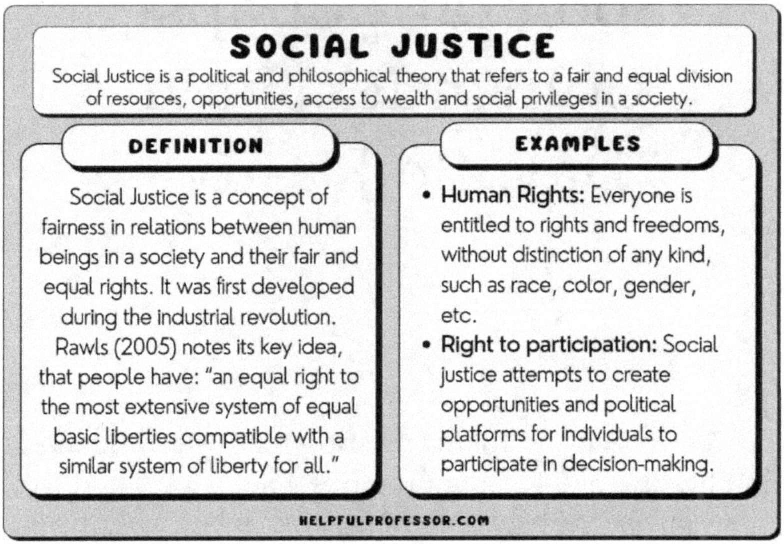

Chapter 13

Societal Collapse Continues Each Day, Be Ready!

January 30, 2024

We live in world that constantly tells us how much of nothings we are. Living in the U.S. I am confronted with this each day. As I live in a country of extreme wealth, millionaires and billionaires who use media to make it known to the world how little we are to this country and world and the impact they make each and every day.

Billionaires Rule our World, Media and Attention

I see billionaires like Musk and Bezos who make it know they have everything one could want in life, fame, power, money, intellect, and we the normal folks are nothing in comparison to them and our lives will NEVER amount to anything EVER compared to them. They are of course not the only people in this country and world who want the world to know how great they are.

I know we live in a world of self-promotion, influencers who pose as caring, but often care about the mighty buck, getting paid at whatever the cost.

I look at these people and I look at these people and although in the U.S. alone there are over 300 million people, I am just one which is nothing compared to. Most many not care about this as one can say I am just trying to live MY life, MY way and no one cares about my life other than myself.

But I truly believe we have set a dangerous precedent of elevating these people in society. For example, I am sick and tired of hearing, reading, and seeing media on the Kardashian, their family and friends, who hog up our news feeds. I get that I can keep strolling, ignore and move on, but its not as easy. Each day we are inundated with peoples lives, living their best lives and although again many will say well what is wrong with that, they are sharing, to each their own, keep strolling and ignore but for many its not possible.

Sick with Politics

What happened to being focused on improving oneself, reading, writing and the basics of making us better humans. That is why I write, I read, I work to improve myself and see every day our loss to what is important today. As we are now in the political season, TRUMP hogs the airwaves, BIDEN, HALEY, and the list goes on as we are forced to hear them talk incoherently about their issues, spreading their hate, anger at society, disagreements with how our country is being run like they can do better.

Truthfully, we are under an illusion that LIFE is and will get better although I hope it will, but wont because MAN or WOMEN are flawed, self-absorbed, greedy and for those who have everything that need in this life like money, why would they care about the No bodies.

We have a lot going on in our society that affect people every single day like homelessness, Hate, Crime, lack of care for society, Increase in suicides each year and basically being able to survive , when many are struggling just to make it while we look around and seeing many SUPER prosperous while others who work two – three jobs to put food on the table, to prevent being on the street as rent sky rockets , food prices are becoming out of touch and our families are suffering when we shouldn't have to. Living in California I see that EVERY DAY and No it's not that easy to pick up and leave especially when I don't work a remote Job but do work for global company.

I Have Failed

I am tired, frustrated filled with despair for my family who I am failing as a father, where I truly do feel I am better off no longer in this world, allowing my family to cut my dead weight so they could live a better life.

I have now begun thinking more of my daughter's future and what that looks like, being that she is eleven and one day will be eighteen and on her own and thinking of my Wife, who in my opinion have severely let down for working hard each day since marriage but not providing her the life I promised and hoped for her and us.

Celebrity Obsessed

As we continue to a more celebrity obsessed culture, people continue to mimic the rich and famous, even going as far as cosmetic surgery to look like their favorite star, some spending hundreds of thousands of dollars to make it happen, which I find preposterous. When will we as society learn, when we focus on that things that have meaning. How does focusing on celebrities, wealth, the rich help us and I know some of you may say well I like just to imagine that kind of life and not be obsessed and that's ok.

Media Rules Our World!

I think we are mindlessly just too focused on media today as I grew up in the 80's and 90's, Generation X'er here as there was no social media , CGI, AI or anything that could be used to manipulate us into believing in realities that do not exist, self-obsessed . WHERE IS GOD? And I don't mean to make it sound like GOD is not there, of course he is THERE, but Where is GOD in our lives to focus on what is important. I know we are human; we are flawed people and those who love GOD and JESUS get wrapped up in the beautiful, the money, having nice things, living rich beyond our dreams, but there is more to life than money, fame.

Basically, each day we focus on these things, we lose sight of the people in our lives, the loved ones which causes harm to our society and the people in our lives. I think we are also mindlessly following others and not thinking for ourselves anymore, failing to research ideas and thoughts automatically making someone else's views our own without question, that is wrong. We are becoming Lazy in this world, and we are letting people control our thought process, we are losing our original thought and its sad.

People have Stopped Thinking for Themselves

We are on a dangerous path in our world and country as we continue to get worse with book banning, hate, no longer hiding our crimes but out in the open as people have no problem taking what they want, stealing, murdering and causing real harm. But what many may see is those who run our countries, states and local communities act with impunity with their crimes.

I find it sad and interesting that we are so consumed with social media today, looking at others, their fake lives and now with generative A.I. and deep fakes how do we even know what is real anymore. How do we know we are talking to a real person especially online when you have no idea who is on the other end. We are truly in days of

Skynet and again films predicting what is to come, but we are surprised when it happens, WHY?

Not sure if this makes senses, but this was burning in my mind today. RANT OVER!

Chapter 14

American Democracy is Ripe for Destruction

Original title: American Democracy is Ripe for Destruction As Society is so focused on Taylor Swift.

February 15, 2024

We are ripe for a takeover in the good old U.S. as the future president will be decided this year. Which is normal for our country, but not so much as we start to see the tides are shifting to installing potentially a true populist authoritarian into our country for the first time.

We here often look at other countries who experienced similar situations electing those who take over the country and pillage it. Although NO man or women is perfect but there are those who have tendencies to rule over people with an iron fist, control people and resources.

What I have seen over the course of my lifetime is how people have grown to kiss the ring our leaders today, pledging loyalty and fealty to a man or women and it doesn't just go for political leaders.

Celebrity Obsessed and Sick in the Head

We in the U.S. are sick with obsession over the celebrity, the business leader, political leader and most who have great wealth and physical beauty. Sadly, this is nothing new to our society, it has only gotten worse over time especially with social media giving those people access to the world where they flaunt their wealth, showing society what We do not have and have worthless us peasants are to society.

The Devil is certainly the biggest distractor to us as many are looking away at those things that have no significance or meaning. As our attention is drawn to other things, it will be perfect for something to take place in society that we are not expecting like natural disasters, war, changes in society and government and we are completely unprepared.

One fatal Catasprohe for California and We are Done!

Living in California myself, we would just need one major catastrophe event to destroy our water supply, our infrastructure, our telecommunications, and communication capabilities, we would be sitting ducks.

Again, we are too focused on what doesn't matter in this world. I get it many and most are focused on just trying to survive and major events would shape our lives in ways we can not imagine. We look to leaders in this country to guide, to maintain and to keep the lights on so to speak, but what if those leaders are just self-consumed with themselves and what they get forgetting about the people.

I cannot speak for everyone, only myself but people in politics and business who have wealth and power will not be affected by devastations because they can always go somewhere else, like their private islands or bunkers. Don't get me wrong, I know we will and have always had rich, powerful people and they have always used their influence, but it seems now its much more transparent with social media that one's dirty deeds are exposed to the world.

We Make Others Wealthy While We Stay Poor

We as society give our hard earned money to Artist, musicians , movie stars, politicians, business leaders so they can become rich, live their best lives while society struggles just to put food on the damn table and not become homeless, but yeah let's see what Elon Musk and Bezos are doing on their yachts and how they spend their billions while many in U.S. have no food to eat tonight, living in poverty.

When will we wake up. GOD is the only one who cares, but people often say if GOD cares why do we suffer?

We suffer because we ALL live in sin. We Suffer because Adam and Eve defied what God said and, in the end, we are here because Adam and Eve. We can all live good lives if we seek the Lord, but we must because he has already told us what will become of this world, but many do not want to believe he has foretold it.

Our World is Dying

We live in a sick world, that is dying each day but when will we see that. Life is precious to GOD, but he has a better place for us in heaven and living in eternally but sadly many go to hell in disbelief. For Jesus has built his kingdom with many mansions.

The Devil Rules This World and Many Follow Him

The Devil rules our world right now which is why people are so consumed with greed, hate, anger, fifth and debauchery and will only get worse as we continue to hate our fellow man, women, and child. I see each day at our borders, how Society hates the migrants who only wish to survive and can not because their home country has stopped caring, turning their back on their own people.

In the U.S. we are consumed with hate for people we will never know and act as if there is NO ROOM AT THE INN mentality, when there is room. They are not taking our jobs, they are taking the job NO one Wants as they clean your toilets, wipe your Ass, Cut your grass for fractions of the cost. They are not running billion-dollar companies, they are NOT your manager, they are taking care of your children for peanuts instead of hundreds or thousands of dollars.

Migrants are NOT the Enemy

As someone who has known the migrant, many are humble honest people just trying to feed their families and be ok. They are not murderers, rapist, drug dealers, they are families who just want to live in Peace, but here in the U.S. that is not allowed until they show us their papers, acting as Mini-Gestapo's who demand from others we have NO right demanding from, because we are NO one, You are NO one to ask or demand from others.

FOLLOW JESUS FOR THE LOVE OF GOD

Instead in the words of Jesus, love thy neighbor like you Love yourself, because YOU LOVE yourself more than anything as we greedy for LOVE for ourselves so why is it so hard to love others. True Love comes from GOD, but again many choose not to follow GOD, they wish to live without him and just go at life alone although GOD is omniscient, knows that past , present and future and already knows what will happen to the U.S. but it would be great to have the inside track as GOD does show us believers.

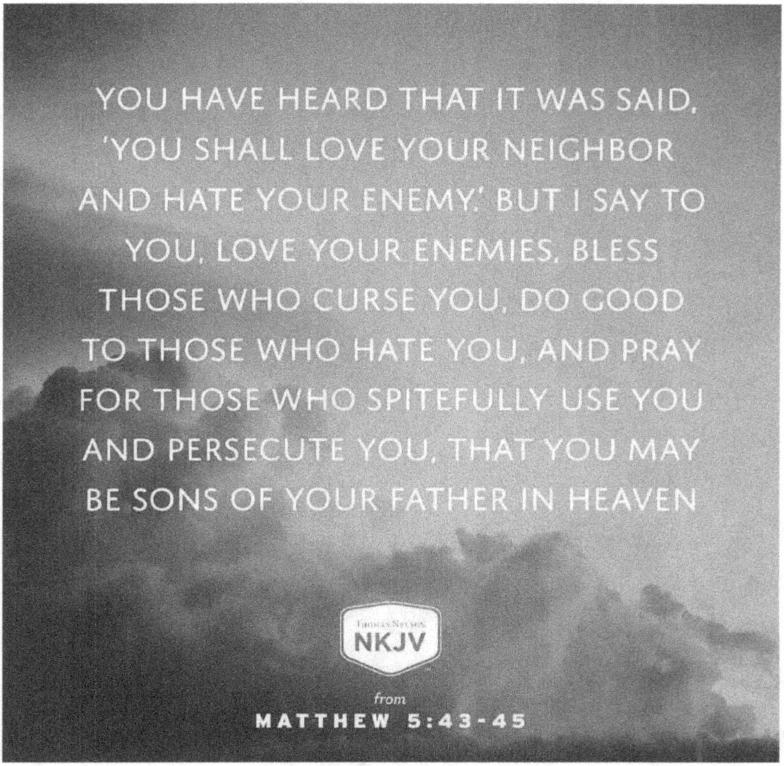

Continue to let the devil distract you, confuse you but to each their own I guess has GOD gives us free will, which is great, but many choose the wrong will, path which leads to damnation.

For some reason I am unsure why I feel triggered today, I guess seeing the countless images of Taylor Swift, Kelce and their fantastic life as they travel the globe, making millions with the world at their feet, but again to each there own.

We can NEVER say we were not warned about what it to come in this society as we are ripe for dictatorship, loss of freedoms and full blown 1984 redention predicted by Orwell, GET READY FOR HELL ON EARTH.

Chapter 15

Christian Nationalism The Ruin of Christianity?

Original title: Is Christian Nationalism The Ruin of Christianity? How Politics Has Degraded What Jesus Meant.

February 24, 2024

With a New future President or potential Dictatorship coming to America this November. Christian Nationalism has been in the news lately as future presidential candidates pine for the Christian right. As a Christian I find it disgusting that the name of Jesus is used as a prop to get ones agenda passed. Using ones love for Jesus as a means to elect a person into office, the highest office in the U.S and world in a sense.

I ask myself how is it in today's age that Christians can follow anyone other than Jesus all on account that our Christian agenda can be met discounting that JESUS is the maker of what happens in this life and society and only HE has the ability to change things in our lives. Yes Jesus uses each of us but we are NOT god and again I am repulsed how people make a person into some type of GOD and you know who I speak of.

I get no man or women is perfect and I should not suprised of the times we live in as society continues to distruct and get only worse. When I look at those who follow so blindly, its like sheep to a slaugther, as sheep are the stupidest animals to exist.

There have new entries into Christian Nationalism, even a new documentary by Rob Reiner in God and Country, which I have not seen yet.

As a Christian for 10 plus years now I have a strong understanding of what it means to be a Christ follower. I am by no means perfect and I will never claim to be, I sin like every man, women and child in this world even if you think you don't you do. Christianity is extremely sensitive topic to talk about and for some it turns off people lumping Christianity into a bigoted religion whose only intention is to limit people, spreading hate and fear. First and foremost that is NOT Christianity but those who profess to say they are why they hate, be bigoted and only wish to hurt others and churches are filled with those people.

We Are a Christian Nation

I will say this I do believe as a nation we were built of Judeo-Christian Principles and to this day those ideals are still part of our culture and our government, but what I am going to discuss here is something so much more than that. I respect others ideals, beliefs alike and although I am believer in Christ, I believe in treating everyone with dignity and respect. For those who read the bible we are follow what Jesus says and Jesus was about LOVE and his message.

We are all taught as Christians we are all apart of the body of Christ and whose who profess to love Jesus need to live a certain way. The way in NOT perfection but in Love, respect and honor to Jesus and to treat those around us with Love. The bible is filled with beautiful scripture which I consider to be GOD's love letter to us as he truly does love us all even when we as people don't always love him.

One would think that we should all have unity in the church and be one big happy family but unfortunately that is not true. Yes we are a family and like any family we are all different, even having the weird uncle and for the most part whose who truly profess to love Jesus do and I spend my time with those.

But where I have truly seen a shift is the moment the Trump became president as he pushed hard to get evangelicals on his side make promises to gain their vote. Now I am not saying its necessary wrong to vote for a president who appeals to our needs as a person and country in most cases that is why we vote for a specific candidate whose ideals align with ours.

A Shift To Christian Nationalism Under Trump

In Trumps case he has NO ideals, he in my opinion is a cheating, lying , womanizing rapist who has a long history of abusing those around him. For many who hear this I would be called an anti-Trumper and I am ok with that, because deep down I see his game who completely baffles me in how he game evangelicals but I believe I see how and its NOT just him appealing to that base. As a believer we are taught abortion is wrong, be prolife, love Israel, fight for religious freedom which seem to be the biggest issues and I will add the sanctity of marriage between a man and women.

All of these beliefs are not just tied to Christianity, other religions believe similarity but Christianity is by far one of the largest groups with this belief. I am not saying I don't believe that Life is important, of course it is or marriage or having religious freedom and of course we must support Isreal because as a Christian you Can not Say oh I love Jesus and Hate Jews and the Country we Must want and pray for those things.

The problem lies in our culture, our world that unfortunately we are not going to change, although we can try. We can try to set laws to limit abortion or even eliminate it, we could make marriage between a man and women ONLY, we could even create laws to limit the rights of the LGBT community and bring the Bible back to schools. But lets remember we live in a nation of Not just Christians, so we CAN not force other to believe in what we believe and that is why many times whose who fight for Christians and their right lose battles because our courts and laws are geared for all of society not just one sect.

Trump since in office has tried to change that but attempting to put conservatives in the supreme court and federal courts in a way to tip the scales in his favor so when certain cases go to court there is a most likely chance he can win, but NOT always. He is NOT a Christian and it is my belief he could care less about Christians and their beliefs they are just ponds for his re-election.

What is Christian Nationalism ?

He plays on the platform of Christian nationalism. Some of you may or may not be familiar with that term but you are probably more familiar with Nationalism. Nationalism is simply identification with ones own nation and support for its interests, especially the exclusion or detriment of interest of other nations.

So nationalism is in line with Christian Nationalism which is similar in the sense of the following:

Christian nationalism is Christianity-affiliated religious nationalism. Christian nationalists primarily focus on internal politics, such as passing laws that reflect their view of Christianity and its role in political and social life. In countries with a state Church, Christian nationalists, in seeking to preserve the status of a Christian state, uphold an anti-disestablishmentarian position. Christian nationalists have emphasized a recovery of territory in which Christianity formerly flourished, historically to establish a Pan-Christian state out of the countries within Christendom.

Some of you reading this are probably asking so what does this mean and for every country its different, but for the US it primarily focuses on the following:

Christian nationalism in the United States manifests itself through the promotion of religious art and symbolism in the public square, such as the displaying of the Ten Commandments and the national motto "In God We Trust", which came into force in order to distinguish the United States from the state atheism of the former Soviet Union. The Foundation for Moral Law, for example, was founded for this purpose. The ideology also advocates for public policy to be supported by religious beliefs, such as enshrining the sanctity of life in law through the buttressing of the pro-life movement. Christian nationalists support Sunday blue laws in keeping with traditional first-day Sabbatarian principles; the Lord's Day Alliance (LDA) was organized by representatives of various Christian denominations to this end. In 2018, the Congressional Prayer Caucus Foundation began Project Blitz to achieve these goals.

Basically what Christian nationalism is the promotion of Policy which as mentioned deals directly with changing laws, adding conservative judges to the federal courts and in the supreme court. Trump has been systemically picking apart our courts for this reason to make evangelicals happy so they will once again vote for him despite his racism, his narcissism and hate for people of color and women I might add. For many who follow him they will deny he is racist, that he loves this country, that he even loves GOD, but he only loves himself and has only wish to enrich his life through the US government.

I implore others to learn who Trump is but many times Christians are blind to who he is and frankly they do not care as long as their agenda is done.

Why should you care you ask? Well because we are republic of people that's why, we are a nation of immigrants, people in all walks of life, rich, poor, you name it and what I see is he could care less about those who truly need help. I understand that as a nation and a state we have leaders who are supposed to fight for the small guy or gal when people vote them in office and they usually don't and haven't. Trump is the president which makes him the leader of our nation and he has failed us ALL. He has failed especially in this pandemic placing blame on China, on Obama and willing to blame anyone unwilling to be accountable yet Christian Nationalist vote for him.

The Issues Are Important

Do I believe Christians should care about the issues, of course I do. Do I believe we should all VOTE and be apart of the political process, of course. Do I believe in choosing leaders that align with our values of course, but this where I don't agree.

I believe for anyone in office, the person requires a moral compass for a nation to lead, a person who doesn't necessarily need to be in politics but someone who

LOVES people and wants to make a difference in the lives of all man, women and children for the betterment of humanity.

We don't have that unfortunately; we have a fear mongering president with fascist tendencies who loves the attention of dictators like Putin and Kim Jung Ung among others. WE have someone who allows other countries to hack our systems and I believe allow bounties on our US soldiers abroad, in addition to the final nail in the coffin he was Impeached.

Many Christians choose to look the other way all in the name of progress for Christians, when ultimately GOD has the power the shift the powers of man for good or bad. This has all been a lesson for true Christians in who you choose to lead a country. Someone who does NOT lead with love and compassion can NEVER been a true leader. I am not saying Biden, Kanye, Warren or anyone else would be better they are all different but one common factor I saw in all of those Except Kayne is they LOVE people and want to better society. We may not always agree with everything they say or do but at the end of the day they are moral people with a conscience and a moral compass something we need in our lives and the lives of our leader.

Where Should We Stand

Sorry I get off topic but my point is Christian nationalism is NOT the answer, because I will say this policies and laws do NOT lead with compassion and Love in many cases they are used to help only certain parts of society.

Now I love people, I love Christ and only wish to follow him and lead with a love heart for others whether your straight , gay , transgender, Black, white, brown, white whatever you are deserve respect and compassion not to be put down further.

With Christian nationalism is really about our values being placed at the top of the pile and putting everyone's else's ideals and beliefs at the bottom. Our beliefs are NOT more important than yours. Yes I want others to come to Christ, go the heaven, live in eternity. But at what cost. Am I will be vote for some who is willing to toss others aside like a piece of garbage, NO! The only prime example is what has happened in our borders, Detention centers, abuse of children and adults all in the name of building a damn useless wall and living in fear and using hate and racism against who are less fortunate and poor. Yes I get we have laws and yes to a certain degree those who came here illegally broke laws, but does that deserve someone to be abused, have their kids taken away, NO!

Lets lastly go back to WHO Christ is, would he condone or accept what is going on today, I say he would surely hate it and does. We have failed even as Christians to do what is right and unfortunately this is what happens when Christians choose to stop following the bible and choose to follow a man, instead of allow GOD to have control.

I am sick over this, I am tired of turning on the news, seeing in social media and see the destruction that has taken place waiting for Christians to stand up and say

ENOUGH! But none, I hear only silence especially in the border issue. What so infuriating is kids at the border who are innocent being locked up and abused by those in government.

Christian nationalism Does NOT work, believer in Christ, following your bible does, praying works and leading with love and compassion as Jesus commanded. This was placed on my heart in what I see today, I am filled with both anger and sadness over what I see each day in the body of Christ. Only GOD knows what the plan is, will our country recover, get worse, only GOD knows.

Praying for everyone affected in this world, COVID-19 and who struggle with what I do each day. Thank you for reading.

This piece was originally written July 18th, 2020 and revised with today's current cliente.

Chapter 16

The Decimation of Society and Only Getting Worse

February 24, 2024

Let them eat cake, if often repeated as said by Marie Antoinette, but actually history shows it was most likely said by Jean-Jacques Rousseau's confessions in 1765. Who knows who really said, but its often a display that the cares of peasants are not important.

Who are the peasants you ask, well WE of course. The peasants can be the average person who gripes about their problems often by whole societies.

We happen to live in that kind of society, a society that preaches to each their own, a dog-eat-dog world as we are to fend for ourselves and NO one is going help us, we are on our own.

Heatless Society and Getting Worse!

We live in a heartless society that is ok with people failing, not having the necessary food and shelter to survive. Where corporations and their greed infect our lives just to get the necessities like food.

It is said since the pandemic, corporations are the reasons for high prices, High inflation because they felt the need to take advantage and are NOT going to lower prices as they are happy with their greed. We are stuck paying for it as the cost of rent continues to rise, outpricing many who can not even afford a one-bedroom, crappy apartment that isn't even worth the materials it was built it, but what can we do.

Just so you know you are not alone, many are struggling to make it, even those who normally would be fine with double incomes. I personally work two jobs, 1 full time, 1 part time and my wife works too and living in California where the cost continues to rise, I pray we will be ok but at what point do we say enough to caring so much if I bills get paid on time, as long as they get their money, why do we put so much DAMN pressure on ourselves to pay ONTIME. I get it we are condition that we do not want to MESS up our credit, we NEED to be on good terms with creditors, we NEED to be responsible, blah, blah, blah, Thanks mom

There are things that really trigger me, often when I see the wealthy bitch about the cost of living, that they can not possibly live off $200,000 dollars or a million dollars and what are they going to do. I may NEVER make $200,000 in my given year, and if I did, I surely would not be bitching about how the world is unfair to me and my family, just shut the $%&@#$ Up already.

Our society is cold and heartless as we see people just trying to make it and the fat cats of world say, "Just let them eat cake". Let them starve, be homeless, destitute, suffer, what do we care I have everything I need. We even see it today with average Joe's who are not wealthy have a lack, an ounce of empathy for their fellow, man, women, and child that is world we live in.

What's The Point of Worry

What is the point anymore to worry so much about what Society things, what are creditors think of us as it's a business, a faceless entity whose only care is making money however they can get it. Corporations would stripe us of our Livelihood if they could.

Don't get me wrong I pay my bills, because frankly I can not not pay the electricity, the gas, the rent, even the phone and car, we need all of things. But do we need the credit card, that subscription, that bill that doesn't impact anything to our credit, like our cable bill, why do we care if we pay on time. Even paying your electricity or gas bill will NOT result in automatic shut off.

We look around today and see people getting away with murder for not paying their responsibilities like people who don't pay child and spousal support, those people are far worse especially who do not support their children all on account that they HATE the Mother, They say they are NOT the father and refuse to pay.

I think about all those rich people who refuse to pay their share in society, who cheat the system, but I guess you can say society lets the rich cheat the system, but who is going to fight some millionaire or billionaire, its easier to go after easy prey like you and I to get something, who cares if it causes great harm to people.

My Hate of Politics

I am fed up how those who are supposed to be model citizens cheat the systems, like Politicians, because again who is going to fight them as the can literally say and do what they want, which is why I HATE politics.

Some would say there are people who care, that try to help those in need, but there's very little of who care as we MUST focus on ourselves, focus on surviving and doing what we can to Keep the lights on and our ability to go to and from work, where often we put our credit cards ahead of everything instead of paying the rent, instead of putting food on the table, the basic necessities come first instead of worry about the face loan companies.

Stop Feeling Guilty

Let's STOP feeling guilty for putting our basic needs first and not the Loan companies, Credit cards and those that have no ability to put us on the street. I understand we still must pay them, they are due but on your TIME , when you CAN.

Let's wake up, get Angry at the Injustice that takes place each day and its only getting worse. Lastly What I am saying kind of goes against my Moral and Ethical principles, but WHO cares. I know GOD will provide and no where in the bible does it say we need to Fidelity to companies, that we need to kiss their ring.

Chapter 17

Amerika, We Are In For an Awakening

Original title: Amerika, We Are In For an Awakening, Wake up before it's Too Late!

March 5, 2024

Not to be an alarmist but America is under a great threat to our democracy. I am unsure how much the average person things of democracy, our country, the rule of law and the potential for America to be under a dictatorship or have an American Hitler. I hate the world of politics, its divisive, hateful, makes you rage as those in society who we think are supposed to show compassion, respect and intellect rarely don't.

Media, One of The Worst Offenders

The media are probably the worst offenders, drawing on people's rage to tune in, join in on the rage, propping up their ratings filling the airwaves, our newsfeed with garbage. Many will say well just don't look, ignore the noise, which is not easy as it's everywhere.

Book Bans Is Where it Starts

There are certain events that I see in the U.S. that are HUGE red flags to our freedoms, under threat, which seem to be just allowed, something as simple as book bans. For many banning books may not be a big deal, if you are NOT a book reader and choose to get your education online, which is not necessary a bad thing other than the fact that there is a a lot of false information online, that tries to change the narrative of history.

You see, because so many people are focused on online, its easy for someone to write an article, a Wikipedia page, a journal, or other source with false or misleading information on some of the most important topics like history, basically attempting to rewrite history.

Orwells Predictions are Here!

We truly are beginning to look as if our lives are shaping to look like Orwell's 1984 with the thought police and the rewriting of history to fit the agenda of government and of course Big Brother watching, which in a sense we have that already.

Rewriting of History is Here

Again books, tend to be accurate, much like a text book but like any book versions change, words , text are removed and that can be reshaped too. Imagine if you will if books and any source of information omitted that there were ever a Holocaust or Native Americas or any other major world and U.S. events or tragedies like Slavery. In regard to book bans, we were probably close to Fahrenheit 451, another dystopian book as we see Life imitating art and where are the alarm bells for many.

I truly believe there are many who want to live in this prehistoric society of oppression, and in political terms, just to own the left lets take away the rights of people, lets allow anarchy and fill the streets with more hate and just allow people to do whatever they want.

Our Legal System Still intact for Now.

We still have a strong legal system in the U.S. although far from perfect as we have laws for Rich and Poor and the rich rarely have accountability, but the poor of course are punished. How many times do we have to see those in this world and country go unchecked free to commit atrocities basically murder with so much a slap on the wrist where most of us would be locked away, throw away the key.

The danger is real, as I look around especially in California where crime seems to be at an all time high, but its not just in California and its not because of Migrants, Illegals it's the citizens of this great country acting with impunity.

I ask myself many times what is the point, maybe I just give me, act out, act with anger, rage , break the law, treat people like others acts and who is going to stop me from lying , cheating and cheating for myself, others do it , the rich do it and they are allowed why can't I.

What is holding back people when the laws don't keep people accountable, but just allow the behavior to continue. For many I know we are not like that, we are good, hard working people who only want to live a peaceful life.

So Called Christians

What's even more infuriating is the so called "Christians" in name that is, not true believers who preach the name of Jesus only to commit crimes, speak hate, put down people seeing this from many but especially those in high positions of power like government as they use their platforms to spread their message of Christian hate to millions, spreading like a virus.

Christian nationalism is prevalent in our country, which is just a big lie and real Christians know better but fall for the lie that we need to make our country a nation of Christian laws at the expense of taking the rights away from those who do not believe.

As a Christian I am NOT in agreement of taking or forcing people to believe in what I believe, to create some theocracy, that is NOT what Jesus is asking for.

Jesus and God one in the same gives us free will to decide, what you and choose to follow whether you wish to be Christian, Muslim , Buddhist or whatever you choose to believe or not believe, but in Christian Nationalism you are not really given a choice to have laws created in line to your beliefs, What is the point when government attempts to create a theocracy.

Government Overreach in The Name of Jesus.

My concern is not so much Christian beliefs infused into government, but as long as people are not mandated which is something we have been seeing more and more. Again, as a Christian some would say I should want to see my belief system enforced in the U.S. but frankly I don't believe we should force anyone to believe what I believe, we might as well have Sharia Law like other countries have, a forced belief, an acratic rule of law.

I truly believe we in America are ripe for a full-blown authoritarian state of government, an America Dictator. Many would say that would never happen, our laws, our constitution would protect us from that , but not really if government choose to ignore the constitution, ignore the rule of law as we have seen in the past with Trump and other leaders.

I don't want to say its just Trump, although I hate the man with a passion as an immoral and unethical as they come, but people love him, deify him as some messiah, just waiting for him to call himself the next Jesus as he is already saying he was sent by GOD himself to fight for the people of this country as Democrats destroy our country, take away our rights and try to make people more woke.

Democrats are No Better

In reality do I agree with democrats policies, NO, but I am sorry to say they are the lesser of two evils as I have not seen democrats try to inflict laws to take away our rights in the sense of authoritarian tendencies. Yes they do have an agenda for ideas I don't agree with too like promoting the certain lifestyles of certain groups I don't associate myself with like LGBQT communities.

Nothing against those communities, but I believe that I prefer to teach my daughter who those communities are, not in the sense of being bad people but from a Christian perspective, they choose to have a lifestyle that is not our own and I don't wish schools or societies to promote that to her, I need to teach her.

Call me conservative from that perspective, I have some conservative values of tradition, living honestly through hard work, high ethical and moral standards and a biblical perspective.

Americas Hitler is Here!

I only imagine if were to turn into the next Hitler America what that may look like, as the future President Trump would enact concentration style camps for migrants, legal and illegal, build the wall, eliminate services, government help and aid to those in need.

Enact laws to help his fellow cronies of family members, friends and whose who kiss his ring in loyalty and felty all along enriching himself by tapping into government funding leaving many dissolute, even more poor and far worse off probably causing the next great depression.

Again, many would say that would never happen, we have people in place to prevent that like the supreme court, agencies, millions to prevent that, but not if they pledge their loyalty to God Trump out of fear of his raft. States would be shaped differently of course because those are governed independently, but we would still need the federal government.

The Hate Continues

We have seem glimpses of that in the last Trump presidency of how Blue versus red states were treated and that will only get worse as are supposed to the United States of America, but being united is far from who we are as we live in divisive states today where states and their leaders spread hate towards other states like California, when they should really look at themselves for their own failures.

Yes California has its own failures, like the high cost of living, its felty to silicon Valley, Big Money, entertainment state and living in a state of high homelessness and getting worse each year, yeah we have problems and big ones.

Add on to that I truly believe mental health in our state and country are horrible and seemed to have gotten worse when Mental health hospitals were eliminated, which I am in favor of bringing back, this may curb homelessness and allowing more to get the help they need.

Homelessness, Suicides , hate and Anger here to Stay

If we were to go into a dictatorship state, our Livelihoods would be stripped from us, Suicides would increase, homelessness would rise , Anger, hate, Crime would increase exponentially to levels we had never seen before, Moral and ethical decency would disappear.

Even as a Christian knowing that we are going to have times like this in our life, doesn't mean we want to suffer like this, a true test of our faith would be upon us and many would falter.

I guess if you want to look at other countries who rule with an iron fist or even third world countries, we can look to countries like China, Russia, Iran, India and others whose citizens live in state where government controls their ability to survive, to live prosperously but in the end the rich would be ok as the Zuckerberg's, the Musk's, the Bozo's of the world would be fine, but the rest in dire straits.

A.I. is Shaping Us for Takeover

We are ripe for a take over here, as we continue to give more control to world leaders and technology to shape our lives and although A.I is not necessary new to society, its uses of AI will definitely shape people and society, which I am sure will be in the aid of controlling our information, our minds and thought process, which is all going according to plan we continue to give control in other areas of our life, Boy do I miss pre-Social Media, Cell phone days when we didn't have these forms of control and devices in our life.

Lastly some would say I am giving way to much credit to Trump and what he can do, but that is where you are wrong as he have putting put into place, loyalist like future Goebbels , which in our day and age was Steven Miller, but there are so much in the woodwork he would bring out to bring pain to America and be allowed to inflict on the America people because they are true narcist , sociopaths, Psychopaths and all the paths who would be allowed to do so.

But I am hopeful that there would be checks and balances to prevent this like the Senate, but again if the House of representatives and the Senate win Republican, MAGAT support then we are done for, so be warned.

No Thanks to Regimes

For those are in support of the republican regime and tell me know I should keep an open mind, to accept ideologies of conservatives and MAGA's I say no thanks as so far you have proven to be untrustworthy of caring about the needs of the people.

I get that we want to live in a fiscal responsibility society and haven't been with our 34 trillion-dollar debt, taking things that people need away like social services, food, medical is NOT the answer, this only pushes whose most vulnerable to the brink of homelessness or worse pushing them to death.

I get Dems and Republicans both sling crap at each other but the doesn't make it right, but I guess that's Politics right, to eat your own, Get your pound of flesh to get whatever you want and at whatever cost. We all have a lot to learn to be a better, more compassionate society, to frankly be more like JESUS.

Chapter 18

Gangs, Drugs and Migrants

Original title: Gangs, Drugs and Migrants : Why the Medias Portrayal of Migrants is Way Off and People Believe It

March 9, 2024

The Hate for the Migrant

The hate for the migrant is real and only getting worse in the U.S. and around the world as people look to greener pastures to survive, have a better quality of life and support themselves and their families. I get that in today's media, they are painted as criminals, law breakers, rapist, violent thugs who come through our borders Illegally as people use the word's "Infested, Vermin" as talking points to gain political points within the U.S Election season.

I get it, there have been and will be people who come into the U.S. illegally and commit crimes, but for the most part they migrants are good people.

The struggle for Migrants is Real

I am very connected in a way to the struggles of the migrants and those NOT born in the U.S. as some may call me a sympathizer to those Illegal migrants we hear on the news almost every single day.

Now with political season in full swing, The Right and Left bring special attention to our borders, causing panic to society that those who enter our borders are out to get us, take our jobs, cause crime, kidnap our children, rape our women, and destroy our cities.

Maybe as you are reading this, you may be saying YEAH that is what they are doing now but have NO real evidence this is happening in your life, only believing what you see the media blast on your Television and across your Phones and Tablets.

The Media Cares Noting , Just Ratings

The media is a valuable resource without a doubt, and it is needed to get facts out to the people, but there are those medias that only want to get ratings, lie to the people, cause division, and hate in this country like FOX and don't get me wrong CNN is no saint either.

The U.S. and its people have grown to believe that the migrants are the enemy and in a way who could blame people, but I would think that we were smarter than that, but apparently not, Americans are idiots to believe the lies. Some of you reading this may think I am the one who disillusioned to what is happening in the U.S. with the migrants, illegal immigration but forgot that many of those individuals have no real contact with most of us.

My Connection is Direct

Personally, I am connected, because my wife is Salvadorian whom I love and came to U.S. Legally with a visa but is well vested into what is happening in her home country such as the President, The removal of the violent killer gangs, you know the ones the U.S. deported.

El Salvador, a small Mighty Country

El Salvador a small country ravaged by gangs, murder, and violence, considered to be the murder capital of the world. But with the current president Bukele, a young millennial who has turned around the country for the best.

The Infestation of Gangs

For those not familiar with the gangs in El Salvador with two major gangs the 18th street and Mara Salvatrucha , both rival gangs who have destroyed the lives of El Salvador. There is an estimated over 70,000 gangs, many of which have been locked up recently over orders from the president Bukele.

The U.S. is the true Cause

Mara Salvatrucha also known as MS-13 is an international criminal gang that orinated from Los Angeles, California in the 1980's. Originally, the gang was set up to protect Salvadoria immigrants from other gangs in the Los Angeles area. Over time, the gang grew into a more traditional criminal organization. In 2018, the gangs US membership of up to 10,000 accounted for less than 1% of the 1.4 million gang members in the United States.

U.S. Born Gangs Born and Raised

The other rival gang called 18th street gang, also known as Calle 18, Barrio 18, Mara 18 or simply 18 is a multi-ethnic organization that started as a street gang in Los Angeles. It is one of the largest transnational criminal gangs in Los Angeles with 30,000-50,000 members between the U.S, Mexico and Central America and is also allied with the Mexican Mafia, another US based crime organization.

The 18th street gang formed in the Rampart District of Los Angeles in the 1960's by Mexican Americans and other Immigrants who were not accepted into existing gangs. Expanding membership into other nationalities and races.

Two killer gangs that started very similar in Los Angeles, my hometown of all places, and what is amazing is that we here in the U.S. act as we were nothing apart of the pain inflicted on those arounds the world.

Since Bukele came into power he has cracked on gangs, arresting over 75,000 having affiliations, which has overcrowded El Salvador prisons and has led to the country have the highest incarceration rate in the world by 2023.

President Bukele is Taking The Country Back

President Nayib Bukele has been criticized by human rights groups outraged over the arrests and the U.S expressing concern about the violence in the country and the methods used to combat it. Now other countries and politicians across Latin America in countries such as Chile, Columbia, Costa Rica, Guatemala, Honduras, Educator and Peru have implemented similar security measures.

I often think what problems we have here in the U.S. as we continue to have gangs that take hold of cities that have been around for decades and although we do not hear about them each day, because frankly the news doesn't wish to report a problem we have had for decades. We do have high crime rates, especially in California.

Gangs Infest U.S. Society Today

Having grew up in Los Angeles, the ultimate gang territories especially where I was from South Central, horribly crime infested with good hard-working people, who many happen to be Latino and many to be immigrants just trying to make it, only imagining what they may be thinking probably having from countries with high murder rates.

We are a nation of migrants which many forget, and it truly believe we still are but a nation who prefers to except migrants anywhere other than Latin countries, fully accepting of migrants from Europe and rule out Asian countries.

The Influx of Migrants is Nothing New

Countries where we have seen the biggest influx over years, but decades is our neighbors Mexico, Nicaragua, El Salvador, Ecuador, Honduras, Guatemala, Panama, Costa Rica, Venezuela, Cuba, Haiti, and the list goes on. The right-wing media loves to paint migrants as murders, criminals who are out to get us and our jobs, with words used such as "Infest" as if they are subhuman, not people who deserve kindness, respect and love.

Yet people today will often question, well WHY? Why can't those immigrants stay in their country, its Not our problem to take on the world's migrants. Our country is Not the only country that has immigration, but we are often the country that gets it blasted in the news the most especially during the political season.

Its easy to get wrapped up , as you walk down the street, go to your jobs and spend time outside to grow a hate for anyone different, often those from Latin descent, which has lead to hate crimes where people have been felt justified to say horrible things and acts against migrants. We are only getting worse but for many we don't spread or practice hate, but sadly our country is being known for that.

Yes, there is a problem, but not with the people sincerely trying to live better lives, feed their families, with nowhere to turn as their own countries have failed them, unable to help them and unwilling at times. We are one of the greatest countries in the world for a reason simply because we have resources that help people with plenty.

Yes, We have our Own problems

I know some will say well there is NOT enough for all these people they are taking our food, our resources and NO they are not. Yes State municipalities, local governments help them with housing and food at times, but that is a small cost. I do often see the argument that WELL WE

HAVE OUR OWN PROBLEMS HERE, Why aren't those issues being addressed, like homelessness, drug epidemic , Violence, but in reality there are Far more violent U.S. citizens, who go on to kill, murder, Steal and harm it own society with prisons filled those people, yet we don't talk about them, we don't shine a light on them as if those criminals deserve kindness, respect for the harm they have done, but in a way I get why because in many cases U.S. born non-migrant are linked to families and people they have hurt.

Our Drug Problems are Allowed

Would I want to be reminded in the news if someone killed or harmed people in my life, NO but we have no problem making migrants out to be the patsies and criminals coming over the border at a very high cost of human trafficking, deaths and drugs that come into the U.S. Which do not primarily come from the migrants, but through our ports of entry, on trucks, on planes which we allow. But again, who in media talks about those things, just migrants as criminals, gang members and rapist.

I get there are bad actors that come over into our country who are migrants, but often far and few and much less than the media says as the sensationalize media coverage for ratings.

How the Media Paints Migrants

As we in thick of political season, don't follow the noise, ignore it and follow what you feel to be true based on the facts not what FOX, CNN and NEWSMAX tell you but with your one research form valid sources.

I have nothing against CNN, but they are ratings driven like other networks with more of a democrat spin, left-wing media and FOX and NEWSMAX are pure unadulterated Right-Wing media, pick your poison or don't, do your own research and make up your own mind with the facts, not half-truths and sometimes just lies.

GOD, Owns Everything

I have had more experience with migrants then I thought I would have this point in my life, but I have appreciation and respect for those who fight this life for better things, who come and do no harm to people, but try to live honest lives for themselves and their families. I have remember biblically we DO NOT OWN anything, the U.S. although is MY own, I don't own the U.S. God is our creator he owns every piece of land, clothing, food , money and everything we use each day.

Yes we have private property, that is beside the point, but the US is not owned, the Ocean is NOT owned by man, GOD owns everything and he could allow and what he sees FIT, yet we as citizens act as if we own countries and yes I get we have to protect our borders from bad actors but in reality we have far worse things to worry about like the implosion of what is happen in our country where, immoral and unethical people rule our lives, where our countries may strike us with nuclear war, destroy our ecosystem and infrastructure like electrical grid and water supply, where is the outrage about those things.

This piece was written because deep down we need to see the good in people, that is being lost and see why even in congress, decorum and respect are gone and we as a country continue to follow to path of Rome, and we all know what happened to Rome.

Real Aliens are Here and They Mean Harm

Continue to love your fellow man, woman and children, citizen, or no citizen, but your feel human, because in the end we all bleed red, unless you're a real Alien (Extraterrestrial) which in that case you do wish us harm and I will defend myself against your race who look to wipe us out one day. Real Aliens are not our friends and yes, they exist, and they too are coming for us.

Chapter 19

Glorification of Violence in Media

Original title: Glorification of Violence in Media Only Gets Worse, especially by those considered Mentally ill.

April 18, 2024

I often think about the amount of violence that plagues our society in television, film, music, and media and how desensitized we are. Often when I watch television with ads, there are collages of shows and films that highlight a certain genre like horror.

Watching one the other day there was one on Peacock that highlighted killers and murders and deaths, seeing that American Psycho was used multiple times.

The Love of Horror

I'll admit I've been watching horror movies and violence from a young age, remembering when my father won father of year like myself who was eight years old to see Childs play and my sister who was six to see that movie in the theaters, seeing all the classics Halloween, all the Nightmare of Elm streets, IT , Friday the 13th's and whatever was on at the time. Much of my writing incorporates horror themes with murder, killing , paranormal themes.

But frankly I believe that due to the amount of violence we see, it also becomes acceptable to conduct such acts, but I know it's not. Its never okay to kill , murder or hurt anyone, but with films and television, its almost encourage, especially revenge, thinking of all the Rambo films I have seen over the years, terminators and the list goes on.

Life Imitating Art

When I watch such films and television I also look at the plausibility of something like that could happen, for instance, having never seen the film Scanners, but there was one seen where which is often promoted where the character's head explodes, not possible as far as I know or in Halloween four or five, where again one of the support characters, the father is in the basement fixing the washing machine and Michael just happens to there, taking the abusive father electrocuting him to the point his head explodes, again I don't think its possible but in that instance it could be.

We often root for when murderers like Michael Myers or other protagonist kill bad people, regardless there is still the promotion of killing. I get film and television, this is common and will not change, but at certain points we as a society think its acceptable, Why I ask? Will this ever change and if its not going to change, what effect does that have on society and the mental state of our culture where it will only get worse?

The Body Count Continues to Rise

It seems today people carelessly hurt, kill others without a second thought, which just goes to show you the Lack of God in their lives. Its as if harming others is acceptable and the best option to getting what we want and that is not the answer, it sickens me.

I have seen and believe this causes our society mental harm seeing it myself as the images hurt and affect me negatively. One could say well just don't watch, ignore it, move on, but its not that easy.

I feel this sense of sickness at times when I write my fictional stories to add great amounts of gore as these are thoughts already in my mind.

Even looking at some of my stories when I was twelve I would often write short stories about death, killing, monsters, cannibalism and the list goes on.

I know for some it is just fiction, doesn't exist in real society, but if anything minds of susceptible to harm especially now with social media.

One of the films that for some weird reason I identify with and like is "The Joker", but what I like about that movie is not the violence, but that sadness of a broken man, who was forgotten about, a mentally ill man, who many would consider just crazy, a psychopath and maybe he is, but I would like to think he got there for a reason if you were to examine is childhood and life.

I get it, it's just a movie, not based in reality, but then coming soon is Joker 2, with both the Joker and Harley Quinn who are psychopaths. What I find interesting is that film and even society try to create sympathy for these characters, and even at times find acceptance in what they do, on account, they are both broken people, but at the end of the day they are still allowed to survive to live their lives.

Mental Illness is Not Funny and Not for your enjoyment

It used to be that those who suffered with mental illness were helped and not encouraged to be violent, but today it seems that is acceptable and understandable as people are not themselves.

It is never acceptable in any form, whether one has a mental illness or not to commit acts of terror, violence, murder, or killing just because a person is not sound of mind.

This Behavior is not acceptable

I get this world makes one and can make one crazy to allow this behavior but it's not natural or normal, it's not civil, which is what what people want today.

I guess whatever makes money these days as Joker and I am sure Joker II will be very successful at the box office, only making it seem more acceptable that unstable, depressed, psychopathic clowns run the city and cause havoc and Manheim.

Why are we as a society so surprised when there are mass shootings, murders, and violence in society when we only just seem to encourage this behavior.

I am not saying do away with films, and television, but be more reasonable as media has great influence over the minds of others, especially the young like children and even teens. The damage is real and some may question the effects of today of social media versus film and television violence and they are both bad.

Thinking of our political clowns who make a fool of themselves each day, acting as the real clowns, spewing venom from their months against each other and the people of this country, what can we expect in how we are to act towards each other.

Some may think I'm taking film and media way too seriously and to lighten up but No I will not . We in society have become too accustomed to thinking it's okay to marginalize those in need and those who struggle and suffer in life, they are not a punchline.

Chapter 20

Politics, Faith, and Society

Original title: Politics, Faith, and Society: A Christian Perspective

October 23, 2024

I often think about the innocence of times, being a lover of history and simple times. As of now I am watching "Little House of Prairie", a show that ran from 1974-1983, a show I had never seen before but heard about the incredible writing, storytelling based of the written works of Laura Ingalls Wilder books. Taking place around the 1870s about life in the old west, I time in period I really love, although If I was living in that time today, not sure If I could cut, but would have had.

The show is too damn heartwarming at times, with the ingals family, the town, his friends and life. I mean you watch this show and you can only think, I feel like I am watching television from a time when innocence reflected in television and movies, but that is all gone today, but its okay, times them a changing.

I look at today's times, especially during this election season, where politicians throw insults, fill the space with hate and anger, but I guess thats politics. I'll admit I hate politics, and what it stands for today, where its no longer about doing what is right for the people but doing what is right the person, making their money, self dealing and doing what it takes to WIN. Not only that, once one wins, its not about the people, its about using their time to self deal, make a name for themselves and make their mark on history.

Today we have two candidates Harris versus Trump, two candidates who couldn't be more different. In my opinion one is highly intelligent, college educated and has made a name for herself primirly in California. The other a former president and current business man, convicted felon and ultimate self dealer, who has used almost everything in his power to stay out of prision, where as most of us common folk would be in prison already. The other candidate is different and not always in the good way as stories of her treatment of her staff, her terrible attitude towards them forcing many to just quit. I get that is not uncommon to many workplaces, there are toxic people in every workplace and that doesn't make it right.

The people we elect and that are elected are representatives of the people, for values that represent the people. Yes both canidates may not represent my values, but some do. A christian man myself, one would think I must automatically vote for a man who has the christian confidence and vote, who will defend my religious freedom and protect me prosecution from the people and society and I say that only one person and God will do that, Jesus Christ.

Trump is not my defender or anyone's defender, he will only defend himself from his own prosecution and potentially be put in jail, but the man will NEVER see a jail or prison because we live in society that has two justice systems, one for the rich and one for everyone else, where us commoners will eat it when we d wrong but the rich, the public figures.

There is certainly a culture war today of what society should look like with great focus on women's bodies, having the freedom to be who you want to be whether that is man or women, a born male wanting to be a female or a born female wanting to be male or nothing having a sex at all and society just accepting their choice. As people our choices are our own, but their also choices that battle with a living GOD Jesus, who loves us nonetheless, sinner and all.

I love people for who they are, male and female, straight, gay, or whatever your orientation is. I am not here to judge people for their choices, who am I to judge, but we do have a great deal of judgment in society, harshly unforgiving judgment. The bible speaks of judgment such as in Proverbs 21:2, "A person may think their own ways are right,but the Lord weighs the heart,"

I am imperfect myself to judgment and I have judged others harshly, but often judge myself more harshly for my inadequacies as a father and husband.

This political system, a lot gets thrown around about the future of the country, if we choose Harris, our country will continue to grow more progressive, we will be taken over all illegal immigrants who will take our jobs, lives and livelihoods, turning our towns into more crime infested cesspools.

I can not say I have seen this first hand, but have seen the changes in my own city, the increase in rent, cost of living and the ability to survive, something both candidates claim they will make better, but I highly doubt that and they most likely make things worse, because frankly they have no cares for the middle class, the poor, the ones just trying to make as both candidates are multi-millionaires with no concern or wealth or money.

This country has bigger problems too, like the state of homelessness and mental health and just health in this country, as if we rotting from within.

How can people be okay with such hate and division in a country, with political leaders wrapped up with their own well being, careless about the people they are to represent.

We are definitely headed for trouble in this country, but it has been prophesied that the end is coming and JESUS is the answer. As Christians we shouldn't be surprised at what is happening in the world as the bible speaks of what is coming, but many even Christians fail to see that, but its all foretold.

Yes, the division, the hate, the anger and the disinformation is overwhelming to the point of what are we to believe. How will we as people continue to survive and thrive under these conditions, and how the people are susceptible to great harm, both physically and mentally and who is paying attention that.

People are not okay, I am tired of people living under the illusion that Trump or Harris will make our lives better, they will not and that is because frankly they dont care, why should they care they've made their life, made their money, have the security they need to be okay, while many struggle and suffer each day, who is thinking about those people, no one.

I am clearly conflicted because as a christian man, evangelicals are saying we MUST vote for trump, he is our answer, deifying him as some type of GOD, he is not god, he is by far one of the worst sinners we have seen in an office of trust, but who cares right, he will give us a better economy, make sure laws get passed to enrich his class. Again Harris is no better, she has her own agenda, but who knows what is.

Remember for many of us we are in the fight together, many who are struggling to be okay and that our biggest problem is making sure we are okay, that we have food on the table, roof over our heads and living this life to the fullest. Jesus already knows who he will make the next president, he sees all, although yes we vote for our leaders, he knows the outcome and why the future holds for us and his message is always cling to him, he will comfort and provide for us, no matter what, BELIEVE.

It would be nice to ge back to the innocence of Little House on the Prairie, wholesomeness, but in essence its a television show and there are others that dont reflect the old west in such a positive way like Deadwood, but when I watch Little House, I think of the time this show came on, which was during the time my mother was a teenager, and mother thinking she too watched this show and most likely loved it.

Where this country is headed who knows, but I wouldn't be surprised if Orwell predicted our future, be ready.

Chapter 21

Is America Becoming Like Orwell's 1984?

October 24, 2024

As a writer and a reader, I often find that fictional imitates real life as something one could think is unimaginable to imaginable to our world. In addition to loving books, I also love film which is where many films created are taken from books. One book I surprising have never read until now is 1984 or Nineteen Eight four by George Orwell.

I have only just begun reading the book and have already watched the film with the late great actor John Hurt and Richard Burton. The film gets incredible close to the book so far, I know many of you will probably tell me about the inconsistencies if any. But like I said I have only just begun the book.

What is so incredible about this book so far is the incredible frightening resemblance to the times we live in today. Now mind you I live in the United States and the year is 2020. Our country on the verge of snapping in two as right and left are at hateful odds, its Democrats VS. Republicans, The Haves and Have Not's. Many will say that my comparison is preposterous and there is no comparison as we live in democracy not a authoritative state, but we are not far off if you look at things and where they are headed.

The Age of Trump

We are in the age of Trump and for many of you that's perfectly fine, as Biden will bring destruction to the world and U.S. which I find laughable. I am an intelligent man with an MBA in business, years in business from education to finance to Software I am no dope. I am smart enough to know that history can repeat itself with those in power who will allow it.

We the people the citizens are really at the mercy of those who run the country as we have to go along with whatever changes are made which includes are freedoms or lack of freedoms. Right not it may seem like everything is normal in a sense but everyone is on edge , but hate has amplified in our nation to new levels.

I truly believe that hate always existed in our country, but now people are free to hate and display that hate even so more than, gone is the civility of our world and country. Many are happy to have to be civil and the pleasantry's of being kind to others, caring for others and loving our fellow man.

One of the most stand alone parts of 1984 is something I came across last night which is:

"In the old days (it ran), before the glorious Revolution, London was not the beautiful city that we know today. It was a dark, dirty, miserable place where hardly anybody had enough to eat and where hundreds and thousands of poor people had no boots on their feet and not even a roof to sleep under. Children no older than you had to work twelve hours a day for cruel masters who flogged them with whips if they worked too slowly and fed them on nothing but stale bread-crusts and water.

But in among all this terrible poverty there were just a few great big beautiful houses that were lived in by rich men who had as many as thirty servants to look after them. These rich men were called capitalists. They were fat, ugly men with wicked faces, like the one in the picture on the opposite page. You can see that he is dressed in a long black coat which was called a frock coat, and a queer, shiny hat shaped like a stovepipe, which was called a top hat. This was the uniform of the capitalists, and no one else was allowed to wear it. ***The capitalists owned everything in the world, and everyone else was their slave. They owned all the land, all the houses, all the factories, and all the money. If anyone disobeyed them they could throw them into prison, or they could take his job away and starve him to death.***

When any ordinary person spoke to a capitalist he had to cringe and bow to him, and take off his cap and address him as 'Sir'. The chief of all the capitalists was called the King, *and –"*

If you focus on the passage in bold, we live in a capitalist country and like today the capitalist own everything and everyone else was their slave. Now you and I work for the man may think well I am no slave, but in reality, we are slaves. We rely heavily on organizations to pay us for our labor but ultimately, they have the control. Many capitalists own the land, the factories and all the money. We live in a time of greed, wall street, lobbyist and nothing happens in the world without money.

Who Really Control's Society?

As you know we have no shortage of billionaires and millionaires and many more are born each day in the land of opportunity. Now some of reading this may say well they deserve their wealth who am I to tell them they can't be rich and wealthy. How does another billionaire affect us you say well just someone else owning the world and doing everything in their power to swift the balance of power from the small guy like you and me to know, rigging the rules for their benefit.

If you think that the rich don't rig the system for them you are sadly mistaken as many of them pay little or no taxes, but the argument is well they provide thousands of jobs with companies like Amazon and Walmart, making slaves of their worker to depend on them knowing they will Never have the power of someone like Jeff Bezos.

Now mind you Jeff Bezos is an intelligent man and used his talents to get where he is today but he had lots of financial help such as his parents and venture capitals making him the riches man in the world and getting richer each day.

So once again what does that have to do with Orwell and where we are headed. There are those who will continue to create a class system as in the book which includes the upper class inner party, the middle class outer party and lower class Proles who make up 85 percent of the population and represent the working class. As the government , the party control the population with four ministries: The ministry of Peace, Ministry of Plenty, Ministry of Love, Ministry of Truth.

Like government each ministry has a purpose to keep control over the people, ultimately Big brother Is the one who watches all except the proles but everyone else they are pretty much under control. We do have a form of big brother watching us, listening to us each day and if you think what you write online and in social media posts is not watched or recorded you are dead wrong as companies like Facebook, Google and Twitter willfully sell our information to the government.

Yes we live in free country for now but for how long, this has really been on my mind for a while now and after watching and reading 1984 we are closer than ever to one day falling under one rule which in my opinion we are not out of reach of someone like Trump.

How the Media Rules Our Age

If we truly lived in the age of 1984 I would never be able to write this, Gestapo type men would be kicking down my door and taking me a way to reprogram me or worse yet kill me and incinerate my body. What is incredibly interesting is the amount of Hate for Media in our day in age and I understand why. I know the media is far from perfect, they lie, distort information to benefit their viewers on TV and on print, they are money driven and must do anything to stay in the game.

I will not call the media the enemy of the people because there are bad actors in all professions, we live in a world of profits, capitalism and greed. To stay in the game of life one must do what it takes to keep the customers coming and although most organizations are in a sense honest they are not out of reach to ripping off the public if they had to. When it comes to the media they rely heavily of viewership, ratings and endorsements and if they don't have that they go out of business.

I make every attempt to not watch CNN , Faux News, MSN, or any major media because deep down they all lie, its not right VS left news many times its lets spin our opinions as truth and fact and its NOT. There are factual news media who tell it straight but in all honestly I choose to try to do my own research when finding out facts on the issues. Social Media is another form of media of verges on the edge of propaganda spinning lies to get more likes and RT's.

Our Attempt at Rewriting History

What is interesting to what is going on today and in 1984 is how the Ministry of Truth rewrites history all the time so that no one ever knows what the real history is. This is what Winston Smith does as an editor of revising historical records to concord the past to the contemporary party line.

We as society have a real problem will history because many times our history is not pleasant , but whose history is as we make attempts to erase the horrible things our country has done such as allowing slavery, eliminating native Americans and removing them from their land, add in racism, wars and so much more that many wish to erase like it didn't exist so a new narrative can be written in its place.

I often think of how history books are written today, what has been removed and kept as I have truly been out of grade school for decades now I can only imagine what is taught today in schools. I find no problem is learning about the horrors of what our country has done, but I also know we have done good too but lets stop try to erase history, but if you think about it any way we are similar to 1984.

Reflections

As I continue to read the book I will surely reflect more on our differences of the book and today in our society and where we are headed. Again if I lived in 1984 I surely couldn't even have a blog, have social media or anything that lets me think and express my thoughts. In 1984 there is only one thought the loyalty to the party nothing else and if I am not loyal I am once again reprogrammed or killed.

Imagine all those who try to speak today in our country and world who are eliminated because their voice doesn't want to be heard by heads of states and governments, its not out of place that we one day become a country that will eliminate peoples voices of thought because there is truth to it.

As you can see I have thought seriously about this, I hope you think about it too as we begin to go into new eras of those who will try to quiet us who have thoughts.

Many who read this post may not find this far reaching, thinking that we can never mimic such a fictional world as 1984 , but in reality countries do exist such as this, who make it a point to control the narrative, control information, try to quiet whose who think differently. Although we may not try to assassinate those we disagree with like others countries have shown to do like Saudi Arabia , Russia and even China.

The Attack on The Free Press

In addition many of those countries prevent free press , something that if things continue to go we could one day lose free press. But you say no Joseph its in the constitution we will never lose that, well I will say that we can lose it because when governments stop following their founders original intent and start making up the rules as they go along or discarding laws and rules than it's very plausible to get rid of those freedoms.

Yes if that was to happen there would be literal turmoil in our country even more so of what is happening now such as more protests, which is our constitutional right, but where there is NO constitutional right is looting and rioting, I condone those actions and only take attention away from those who truly are trying to get a message out about injustice.

Just in today's climate with protestors which again I agree are allowed to protest peacefully, but when looters and rioters come out and destroy property, fight with authorities, kill people in the name of justice, complete anarchy. When situations like this happen states and the federal government then feel the need to take action which can be extreme at times, no one should ever have to die to protest yet we see it happening.

I will not say the police involved is perfect, they obliviously have a job to do to perfect the citizens of our towns and states, but some police can take it too far because deep down they feel empowered that nothing will touch them, that is what happens when law and order go out the window and giving so much power to police. Now I understand we need police to protect us from the bad people, but we don't need police to mimic criminals in the name of justice taking a vigilante approach, that is what is making society made.

So again sorry got off topic, going back to 1984 there can be scary differences to how society was once civil, ruled by law and order and slowly became ruled of one man or a group of men or women. In our case corporations rule the working class which would make most of us proles who are the worker bees making up 85% of society.

U.S Government Vs. Orwellian Government

Within our society we have structure of a government in our case of the United States we have three branches the Legislative, judicial and executive. Most of us know this is out we separate powers building a system of checks and balances, something that has appeared to have gone away with this current presidency. Although many will say well the president of the United States has authority to make choices on how he or she chooses use that power and in my opinion that is a flat out NO.

The presidency doesn't not give that person unlimited powers to misuse those branches regardless if they don't like the rules. That is one of the big issues when leaders break those rules and no one stops them, when in reality most of us who break the rules are penalized , put in jail or go to prison why is the presidency any different, it isn't.

The sad fact is that congress is very powerful as well it should be, but they there to protect the citizens of the countries from harm including an authoritative president or leaders but when they choose to not do anything because of loyalty to a person we all fail as a country and more harm is done to our republic.

In comparison to 1984, there are what are called Ministries similar to our branches. In the book there are four ministries which include:

The Ministry of Love

The Ministry of love serves as the interior ministry. It enforces loyalty to Big Brother through fear, through security and repression, as well as brainwashing. In the book this ministry has no windows and is surrounded by barb wire entanglements, steel doors, hidden machine gun nests and guards armed with "jointed Truncheons".

The interior lights are never turned off, it is considered the most powerful ministry, controlling the will of the population. The thought police are part of this ministry. This ministry is misnamed since it is largely responsible for the practice of misery, fear, suffering and torture. In a sense, however the name is apt, since its ultimate purpose is to instill love of Big Brother, the only form of love allowed.

Each of these Ministries or Branches serve a purpose I found quite interesting and if you have never read 1984 I would high recommend to see the incredible prophetic vision Orwell had in 1949 when he wrote this book.

The Ministry of Peace

The Ministry of Peace serves as the war ministry and is in charge of the armed forces, mostly navy and army. The primary principle in this ministry is the principle of perpetual war, using all surplus resources, keeping most citizens in lives in constant hardship, preventing society from learning enough to comprehend the true nature of society.

Perpetual warfare also helps preserve the special mental atmosphere that a hierarchical society needs. What this means is the balance of the country rests in the war, which is in charge of fighting the war, making sure to never tip the scales.

Again the ministry of peace if opposite of its name, since its main objective is in charge of maintaining a state of war. Perpetual war is what keeps the peace and the balance of power in the world, and since the other major powers also use warfare as a means to maintain the status quo.

The Ministry of Plenty

The Ministry of Plenty is in control of Command Economy which is considered an economic system which the government controls and regulates production, distribution, prices and etc. This ministry oversees the rationing of food, supplies and goods. The central theme of Oceania's idea that the poor, ignorant populace is easier to rule over than a wealthy, well informed one. Telescreens often make reports on how Big Brother has been able to increase economic production, even when production has actually gone down.

Once again this ministry is misnamed, doing the opposite and is responsible for perpetual poverty, scarcity and financial shortages. However, the name is also apt because, along with the ministry of Truth, The Ministry of Plenty's other purpose is to convince the populace that they are living in state of perpetual prosperity. In addition this department is in charge of the state lotteries, very popular among proles who buy tickets in hope to win big prizes, which is a vast hope as the big prizes in fact are not awarded at all.

Ministry of Truth

The Ministry of Truth is the ministry of Propaganda. Responsible for any necessary falsification of historical events. This ministry spreads a new language amongst the populace called Newspeak, which, for example "Truth" is understood to mean statements like 2 + 2 = 5 when the situation warrants.

The Ministry of Truth is involved with the news media, entertainment, the fine arts and educational books. Its purpose is to rewrite history to change the facts to fit Party doctrine for propaganda effect. For example, if Big Brother makes a prediction that is wrong, the employees in the Ministry of Truth correct the record to make it accurate.

Looking at these ministries one would think well yeah these are perfectly plausible to a country who wishes to control its people, taking away ones way to learn the truth instead providing the truth they want society to know and if society chooses not to embrace their truth they can brainwash them.

Are we not in a state of brainwash ourselves in our country believing that one party for example Democrats Vs. Republicans and how Republicans preach that they are the only party that can bring peace to the country, smearing the Democrats as being socialist and against Law and Order, and against this and that, but ultimately have shown they are ones who wish to keep control and try to bend the will of the people by controlling what society can and can not do like voting.

One can say well everyone in the US if eligible has a right to vote and yes that is true, but suppression does exist as states run mainly by republicans try to make it more difficult for some to vote especially in minority populated parts of the country doing everything in their power to stay in power.

I know of you may feel I just making up conspiracy theories about our rights but in truth the reason why its not a bigger issue is because we have really our own Ministry of Truth which is the Media who attempts to control the narrative of what they want the people to know about, this is where it gets to Orwellian with our reliance on Media to get what we need and why its so dangerous to take all the media as truth, in truth everyone has an angle right.

Although I live in the United States, the land of Free, nothing is free , there is a cost to it and in our know right we have our own Big Brother watching us use those resources to say in the future well group X used this amount of resources versus Group XY and so we should take way Group X resources and control them.

Such as control which groups can be in power keeping poverty a perpetual part of world and country when we have the resources to solve homelessness for example, but again every state and local government has that power to decide who we can help and not help.

But once again the control is in corporate America as they really choose what society will be provided , what wages they decide to be appropriate to keep certain groups just having enough to barely make it relying on the government for other resources like welfare keeping those classes in place.

Ultimately I think in 1984 its about the classes of people and keeping it organized so that certain classes will rule everyone else, because once you let the proles rule society will truly only start be fair in sense for everyone, we don't live in fair society of world, as it repeated in 1984 "War is Peace" Freedom is Slavery" and Ignorance is Strength" these government slogans.

War is peace is best examined as the government believing the people must believe that war is peace meaning one must tolerate the horrors of war. The idea is that one must make terrible sacrifices in order to have a peaceful nation.

Freedom is Slavery on the other hand is meant to represent the message that the party imparts to the community that anyone who becomes independent of society's control is bound to be unsuccessful. A society that is based on free will result in chaos and the development of society.

Lastly Ignorance if Strength is meant for the citizens to subvert their will and their awareness to accept the contradictions the government puts forth. They are expected to bury the truth and accept irrationality such as in demonstrated in these three statements.

Ignorance is therefore strength as it is the willing ignorance of the people who ignore obvious contradictions. It is this ignorance that maintains the power of the government and the seeming coherence of the society. Its through this ignorance that people can find the strength and live in a totalitarian society where the government oppresses them even while communicating to them how fortunate they are.

How many times do we in society hear our government how great we all have compared to other countries; how much we are provided and what they are doing for us. In some sense government has an obligation to help its citizens, not necessary to be rich and wealthy but to survive.

Governments know the power they have to help their citizens like provide healthcare, food and shelter but in the U.S. will they ever truly do that probably not because that would resemble socialism which our country is clearly again in principle but in a sense we still bail out corporations and agriculture in forms of financial help, so socialism is still part of our fabric whether we see it or not.

The point I am try to making is the many similarities and possibilities of where society is headed and how ultimately we have our form of Big Brother , government watching us, listening to us and even corporation who have taken it upon themselves to watch us like Google, Amazon and Apple, but that's ok because they are multi billion dollar companies that we know we need here.

I am not against capitalist or capitalism its what makes our country great with the ability to have wealthy and a life of freedom, but eventually our freedoms will come at a cost because of control, control is something someone always wants such as government. The question is when control will more be allowed in our lives and what are we going to do about it before turning into the era of Orwellian government control, its not far off.

I appreciate you listening to my deep thoughts on the matter and I know as I read further into the book more enlightenments will take place and I am looking forward to it, but I recommend you read the book, watch the film and see those comparisons.

Chapter 22

The Divide in America: Choices and Consequences

October 24, 2024

We should all be in fear for this country, the good ole U.S. as we are in election year and our democracy. Democracy is a word that gets tossed around a lot, along with another word fascism, a word we know nothing about but if you have followed history, the world is very familiar with countries who have fallen under fascism, dictators and those who wish to control man, women and child with every choice, decision leaving nothing to us.

If we fail to protect democracy and fail to allow autocrats to rule, then we all be hurt. Although I do believe there are many in the U.S. who wish people to placed in

Tyranny especially the poor, people of color, the less fortunate even at the expense that those people would be affected themselves.

The Division of the U.S.

The United States is severely divided, so much so I never realized how divided we had become, because throughout my forty-four years of life, I went about my life, went to school, went to work, got married, raised my child and family never fully seeing the dangers that are in today. Although as a man of God, God has already prophesied what our futures look like, what man and women will do to our world, which only means that Jesus is coming back soon. For those who do not believe, man and women are sinful, wicked and there is no one that is good, yes not one. We are all sinful and all can do great evil, but we are all given free will to choose to do good and attempt to moral.

Being in the U.S. the people choose their leaders, whether that be those in our congress and those who rule the free world. Being that man in inherently evil, flawed and sinful, those men and women can do great harm.

The Choice that will Affect us and the World

This year we choose between two, a man who had been in government for over fifty years, who has served the people as a congressman, vice president and now president. The other a convicted businessman, a snake oil salesman, an adulterer and most likely a rapist. Some who read my characterization may say I am being unfair to the former president, that he is a good man who loves the people, who wants to do good, the clean up the swamp and that what he wants to do is good.

One could say the media just wants you to believe he is bad, but his record speaks for itself, even though millions will say, it's just a witch hunt. I get our current president is not perfect, flawed and a man who has also made bad choices politically speaking during his time in congress. But there are vast differences between the two men, aside from their age, which they are both old, ancient baffling me as to why we as a country can does not choose a man or women of younger age.

I am not necessarily saying they need to be specifically young, but a man or women of experience. We have had men and young, who were rather young, experienced in office, like JFK and even Obama, Clinton. Although all men are flawed, at least with some sense of youth, they were current in knowing what the needs of the people were. I can not stress enough men and women are never perfect, but there are those who wish to do good to society and not take advantage, not to oppress people.

I would never say who to vote for, that is your choice, but choices have consequences for all of us and we must choose the lesser of the evil. We must choose those who wish to help society, make it better not worse. Although we don't know the future, but I know who holds the future and whatever the future may be, we will all need to accept that it's based on our choices, you've been warned.

I will say that art imitates life, as many of the most incredible fictional geniuses have warned us of our futures, Orwell being one of them of course, just watch or read 1984.

It's time to wake up to what's coming, and it's not good. Not to be a fear monger, although I would love to be positive that everything will work out for the best, but this time I am not too sure. Don't ignore the noise but tune out the noise of the lying media who only wish to confuse you, to get ratings and money. Let's not all the media to choose who this country is led, but unfortunately, I feel this has already happened.

Chapter 23

Threats to Democracy: A Call for Awareness

October 24, 2024

Not to be an alarmist but America is under a great threat to our democracy. I am unsure how much the average person things of democracy, our country, the rule of law and the potential for America to be under a dictatorship or have an American Hitler. I hate the world of politics, its divisive, hateful, makes you rage as those in society who we think are supposed to show compassion, respect and intellect rarely don't.

Media, One of The Worst Offenders

The media are probably the worst offenders, drawing on people's rage to tune in, join in on the rage, propping up their ratings filling the airwaves, our newsfeed with garbage. Many will say well just don't look, ignore the noise, which is not easy as it's everywhere.

Book Bans Is Where it Starts

There are certain events that I see in the U.S. that are HUGE red flags to our freedoms, under threat, which seem to be just allowed, something as simple as book bans. For many banning books may not be a big deal, if you are NOT a book reader and choose to get your education online, which is not necessary a bad thing other than the fact that there is a a lot of false information online, that tries to change the narrative of history.

You see, because so many people are focused on online, its easy for someone to write an article, a Wikipedia page, a journal, or other source with false or misleading information on some of the most important topics like history, basically attempting to rewrite history.

Orwells Predictions are Here!

We truly are beginning to look as if our lives are shaping to look like Orwell's 1984 with the thought police and the rewriting of history to fit the agenda of government and of course Big Brother watching, which in a sense we have that already.

Rewriting of History is Here

Again books, tend to be accurate, much like a text book but like any book versions change, words , text are removed and that can be reshaped too. Imagine if you will if books and any source of information omitted that there were ever a Holocaust or Native Americas or any other major world and U.S. events or tragedies like Slavery. In regard to book bans, we were probably close to Fahrenheit 451, another dystopian book as we see Life imitating art and where are the alarm bells for many.

I truly believe there are many who want to live in this prehistoric society of oppression, and in political terms, just to own the left lets take away the rights of people, lets allow anarchy and fill the streets with more hate and just allow people to do whatever they want.

Our Legal System Still intact for Now.

We still have a strong legal system in the U.S. although far from perfect as we have laws for Rich and Poor and the rich rarely have accountability, but the poor of course are punished. How many times do we have to see those in this world and country go unchecked free to commit atrocities basically murder with so much a slap on the wrist where most of us would be locked away, throw away the key.

The danger is real, as I look around especially in California where crime seems to be at an all time high, but its not just in California and its not because of Migrants,

Illegals it's the citizens of this great country acting with impunity.

I ask myself many times what is the point, maybe I just give me, act out, act with anger, rage , break the law, treat people like others acts and who is going to stop me from lying , cheating and cheating for myself, others do it , the rich do it and they are allowed why can't I.

What is holding back people when the laws don't keep people accountable, but just allow the behavior to continue. For many I know we are not like that, we are good, hard working people who only want to live a peaceful life.

So Called Christians

What's even more infuriating is the so called "Christians" in name that is, not true believers who preach the name of Jesus only to commit crimes, speak hate, put down people seeing this from many but especially those in high positions of power like government as they use their platforms to spread their message of Christian hate to millions, spreading like a virus.

Christian nationalism is prevalent in our country, which is just a big lie and real Christians know better but fall for the lie that we need to make our country a nation of Christian laws at the expense of taking the rights away from those who do not believe.

As a Christian I am NOT in agreement of taking or forcing people to believe in what I believe, to create some theocracy, that is NOT what Jesus is asking for.

Jesus and God one in the same gives us free will to decide, what you and choose to follow whether you wish to be Christian, Muslim , Buddhist or whatever you choose to believe or not believe, but in Christian Nationalism you are not really given a choice to have laws created in line to your beliefs, What is the point when government attempts to create a theocracy.

<u>Government Overreach in The Name of Jesus.</u>

My concern is not so much Christian beliefs infused into government, but as long as people are not mandated which is something we have been seeing more and more. Again, as a Christian some would say I should want to see my belief system enforced in the U.S. but frankly I don't believe we should force anyone to believe what I believe, we might as well have Sharia Law like other countries have, a forced belief, an acratic rule of law.

I truly believe we in America are ripe for a full-blown authoritarian state of government, an America Dictator. Many would say that would never happen, our laws, our constitution would protect us from that , but not really if government choose to ignore the constitution, ignore the rule of law as we have seen in the past with Trump and other leaders.

I don't want to say its just Trump, although I hate the man with a passion as an immoral and unethical as they come, but people love him, deify him as some messiah, just waiting for him to call himself the next Jesus as he is already saying he was sent by GOD himself to fight for the people of this country as Democrats destroy our country, take away our rights and try to make people more woke.

Democrats are No Better

In reality do I agree with democrats policies, NO, but I am sorry to say they are the lesser of two evils as I have not seen democrats try to inflict laws to take away our rights in the sense of authoritarian tendencies. Yes they do have an agenda for ideas I don't agree with too like promoting the certain lifestyles of certain groups I don't associate myself with like LGBQT communities.

Nothing against those communities, but I believe that I prefer to teach my daughter who those communities are, not in the sense of being bad people but from a Christian perspective, they choose to have a lifestyle that is not our own and I don't wish schools or societies to promote that to her, I need to teach her.

Call me conservative from that perspective, I have some conservative values of tradition, living honestly through hard work, high ethical and moral standards and a biblical perspective.

Americas Hitler is Here!

I only imagine if were to turn into the next Hitler America what that may look like, as the future President Trump would enact concentration style camps for migrants, legal and illegal, build the wall, eliminate services, government help and aid to those in need

Enact laws to help his fellow cronies of family members, friends and whose who kiss his ring in loyalty and felty all along enriching himself by tapping into government funding leaving many dissolute, even more poor and far worse off probably causing the next great depression.

Again, many would say that would never happen, we have people in place to prevent that like the supreme court, agencies, millions to prevent that, but not if they pledge their loyalty to God Trump out of fear of his raft. States would be shaped differently of course because those are governed independently, but we would still need the federal government.

The Hate Continues

We have seem glimpses of that in the last Trump presidency of how Blue versus red states were treated and that will only get worse as are supposed to the United States of America, but being united is far from who we are as we live in divisive states today where states and their leaders spread hate towards other states like California, when they should really look at themselves for their own failures.

Yes California has its own failures, like the high cost of living, its felty to silicon Valley, Big Money, entertainment state and living in a state of high homelessness and getting worse each year, yeah we have problems and big ones.

Add on to that I truly believe mental health in our state and country are horrible and seemed to have gotten worse when Mental health hospitals were eliminated, which I am in favor of bringing back, this may curb homelessness and allowing more to get the help they need.

Homelessness, Suicides , hate and Anger here to Stay

If we were to go into a dictatorship state, our Livelihoods would be stripped from us, Suicides would increase, homelessness would rise , Anger, hate, Crime would increase exponentially to levels we had never seen before, Moral and ethical decency would disappear.

Even as a Christian knowing that we are going to have times like this in our life, doesn't mean we want to suffer like this, a true test of our faith would be upon us and many would falter.

I guess if you want to look at other countries who rule with an iron fist or even third world countries, we can look to countries like China, Russia, Iran, India and others whose citizens live in state where government controls their ability to survive, to live prosperously but in the end the rich would be ok as the Zuckerberg's, the Musk's, the Bozo's of the world would be fine, but the rest in dire straits.

A.I. is Shaping Us for Takeover

We are ripe for a take over here, as we continue to give more control to world leaders and technology to shape our lives and although A.I is not necessary new to society, its uses of AI will definitely shape people and society, which I am sure will be in the aid of controlling our information, our minds and thought process, which is all going according to plan we continue to give control in other areas of our life, Boy do I miss pre-Social Media, Cell phone days when we didn't have these forms of control and devices in our life.

Lastly some would say I am giving way to much credit to Trump and what he can do, but that is where you are wrong as he have putting put into place, loyalist like future Goebbels , which in our day and age was Steven Miller, but there are so much in the woodwork he would bring out to bring pain to America and be allowed to inflict on the America people because they are true narcist , sociopaths, Psychopaths and all the paths who would be allowed to do so.

But I am hopeful that there would be checks and balances to prevent this like the Senate, but again if the House of representatives and the Senate win Republican, MAGAT support then we are done for, so be warned.

No Thanks to Regimes

For those are in support of the republican regime and tell me know I should keep an open mind, to accept ideologies of conservatives and MAGA's I say no thanks as so far you have proven to be untrustworthy of caring about the needs of the people.

I get that we want to live in a fiscal responsibility society and haven't been with our 34 trillion-dollar debt, taking things that people need away like social services, food, medical is NOT the answer, this only pushes whose most vulnerable to the brink of homelessness or worse pushing them to death.

I get Dems and Republicans both sling crap at each other but the doesn't make it right, but I guess that's Politics right, to eat your own, Get your pound of flesh to get whatever you want and at whatever cost. We all have a lot to learn to be a better, more compassionate society, to frankly be more like JESUS.

Chapter 24

The Church at a Crossroads

Original title: The Church at a Crossroads: Faith vs. Political Loyalty

November 4, 2024

For those who have read my blogs you may have noticed that I write about a variety of topics from Creative writing, Short Stories, Bigfoot and almost anything on my mind. Based on the title of this piece you will see that I am a Christian and take my faith very seriously.

I am far from perfect, so I will start there and I know that. As a person we are not meant to be perfect, only GOD is perfect, despite what people may say that he is flawed because situations in their favor are not happening. GOD and Jesus one in the same are perfect, omniscient , Loving, Patient, knows the Past, Future and

Present and in my view everything is in his control, nothing is in our control .

What triggered this post and yes I will use the word triggered because I truly see the church going in a horrible direction and although its Gods church not Mine nor man, God has surely placed men and women in charge of his church to preach the word of God and save souls. I am not a pastor I am just a Jesus follower who knows right and wrong something that many Christians today don't seem to know the difference.

How I was Triggered

I am absolutely disgusted with the fact that we have "Christians" who follow former president Trump. I have had the opportunity to speak with many through social media primarily Facebook and they are unlike any Christians I have seen before. Many appear convinced that Trump can do no wrong, his lying , cheating ways are no big deal simply because he is doing their bidding such as filling the courts with conservatives , abolishing abortion in society, which in my opinion that will never be abolished, protecting religious freedoms, having a relationship with Israel. All Many agenda points which most Christians fight for. Now don't get me wrong they are important to me, but at what cost should those things happen, a loss of morality, a loss of ignoring what Jesus says and what GOD hates, which we have all but ignored in this president.

I truly see them as Sheep and although many who read this will see religion in general flawed and that is because Christians are meant to represent goodness but failed and are failing to do that. I am NOT saying there are no good Christians out there, are obliviously are and those who fight for the voiceless. But as a Christians how can you explains how people are treated today. I have faith in my GOD Jesus because he has NEVER let me down, but I refuse to treat people like they don't matter of any race, color , sex and creed, every man and women matters so how is that many today treat others like 2nd class citizens and this goes for minorities too.

I am appalled at how evangelicals have treated those in need like at the border, even the homeless where are they today? where are those fighting for the voiceless and yes I mean the unborn but what the kids at the border who are being abused as we speak in detention centers, who got stripped from the parents and pawned off to foster care which in my opinion is like kidnapping. If you are not aware what happens when an undocumented person crosses the border and caught, the child is separated from the parent and basically given to foster care were others adapt them while we deport the parents back to their country, OH its happen as we speak. I am angry as you can see as we have come to a point that Christians have been consumed in politics Right VS left, Hate.

What GOD Hates

As a Christian I am too have strong convictions about hating evil and GOD is very specific that we are to HATE what he hates which include the following from Proverbs 6:16:19

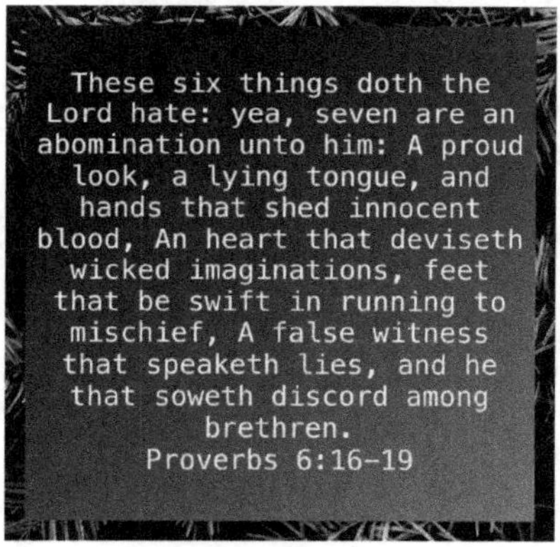

These 7 things the Lord Hates and I do everything in my power to say clear of what GOD hates, again I am not perfect and we all fall short in the glory of GOD, but he gives us specific standards to follow.

You may be asking where is all leading to, its leading to how many Christians today do not even resemble what god hates and those who even follow hate. I see every day especially in the United States who professes the name of Jesus yet does all of these things.

I see it in the church when they proclaim they love Jesus yet they are completely silent on some of the biggest travesty's happening in our country especially those who follow President Trump, a man I personally didn't vote for and would have never voted for due to a man I have seen as evil and who could care less about anyone than himself and time and time again has proven that.

It angers me when I see Churches, evangelical leaders support and continue to support a man who has caged Men, Women and Children without an ounce of humanity or dignity. Despite the difficulties of the situation has made things worse.

I will not pretend to understand what happens on the Border, I am sure it's horrific, but these are human beings are not pawns in his political game of hate for the brown man and women. He has also Lied over 10,000 times purposely mind you, continues to cause conflict in the United States and the world. Continues to run to evil and do evil things that are coming to light every day, yet, people still support him spreading hate, increase in violence and unfortunately many of those are so called Christians.

I am Not Bashing Christians, but those who proclaim to be ones and don't follow God's word, these are NOT Christians, they are followers of Man. I will say that I hope many will see the light, but just like in the bible where Sheep were referenced, that is represented by us, because Sheep are considered the stupidest creatures. But JESUS loves us and if we follow him, he will never leave up for forsake us, that is why I continue to follow him, Not Trump, Congress or anyone else.

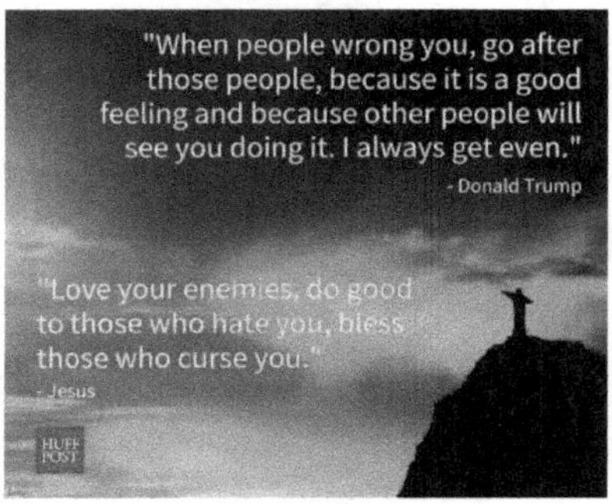

I truly believe times will get worse and they are expected to per the Bible, eventually Jesus will come back for his church and his Bride Groom which is us, but no ones know the day or hour, only he knows.

As a Christian I understand God has a purpose for everything, even placing a man like Trump or any other King or Queen in power, because he has a purpose.

What Jesus Stands for!

Being a Christian can be difficult but worth it, because I know deep down what Jesus stands for is Love, building a relationship with him, following him and loving him. He gives us a choice that will always stand, it is my belief that you can not love two masters, you either are for Jesus or against him, you not have any feelings towards Jesus, so that means to you are against him.

As a Christian I am not here to preach to you, but to love you, be an example of Christian living even though I will fail, because I am man and will fail, but I will always try.

In today's day and age Politics has infused Christianity into that platform, many times spinning God's word to fit the agenda and to make money, two things God surely hates. I see it now and really has always been around, where there will be those trying to make a buck on God's name and people surely fall for it.

I have also seen churches incorporate politics in their messages, not always outright telling us to vote for someone but leaning towards that direction, not giving direct access to other party like Republicans and Democratic candidates. In addition, there is what's called the Christian Elite which are mega churches who have a lot of influence push an agenda and again telling us who we should really root for and I absolutely despise that.

I understand as a Christian we have a mission field to go out and preach the gospel, but what does voting for Donald Trump or another candidate have to do with God's word, in my opinion Nothing.

God Is in control again he will place whoever he wants in power and we will just have to deal with it. It's my educated guess that God will put people in our life for reasons to teach us even if it affects us negatively like Donald Trump who continues to lie, spread falsehoods, self-dealing and really only cares about his base, constantly putting down minorities, Immigrants. Democrats, journalist and anyone who doesn't agree with him.

Again God is in control, so only he knows what the future holds, because we live in republic we have choice which is of course wonderful, but choices have consequences when we make mistakes just like in life.

As a Christian, I live my life devote to Christ, My wife , Daughter, Family who are the core of my life, God Comes first and what he wants for my life.

Getting to the end you may be asking what is the point of this blog, the point was to simply release this burden on my heart over what I see is a sad state of affairs in Christianity in the United States. I say the United States because in certain country's being a Christian is deadly like countries such as Iran, China, even Russia, because the Bible is considered controversial for its principles, where these governments are so afraid of an uprising and people opening their eyes to the truth. It is written Jesus will account for those places that have little or no access to the word of God before the end of days.

I pray the country does turn around fast, our churches as well, but most importantly you and me who will open our eyes to what is happening around us. Of course we are to Live our lives, be busy unto the Lord until his return, not to Fret or do not be afraid which is mentioned 365 times, meaning we are not to be afraid each day of week, because again he is in control.

Again this is not to bash Christianity, its to shine a light on those who profess they Love God, but don't reflect anything godly but worldly, that goes to the Government, those in the church and of course the world. It's time to wake up Christian, open your eyes to what's happening and stop falling for lies of the enemy, pray more, open your bible more, put the phone down and focus on building godly god fearing lives.

In today's society I was against social media for so many years like Facebook and Twitter for the same reasons I am today its divisive, it sucks you to be negative and that goes for be a Christian. Christians are hated online and sometimes it becomes overwhelming to be online but I love the interaction for my writing.

There is some truth online but we have to be very careful and there is lots of misinformation but there is also truth to how people especially Christians act and are silent on important human rights issues.

For those who follow me online you will see that over the past few months I have gotten very political in my posts against our current administration but many evangelicals follow him like sheep in my opinion. He goes against everything Christ stood for. Yes Christians want to abolish abortion , put the bible back in schools and so many other things. Many take choose to have a platform to hate in the name of Jesus because they feel they can justify it but they can not.

Jesus was called for us to LOVE not hate, he was called to die for our sins yet Christians seem to be the best offenders at times especially from what I call the Christina Elite, those mega churches who feel they own Christianity and their voice is what matters. GODS word is what matters, man will always be weak and have self interest even if you are a pastor of a major church, ONLY Jesus is selfless.

Over the last few months I have grown increasingly angry over what I see happening in the church today and even by those who call themselves believers. Now I am by no means a perfect person and I am NOT self righteous in my pointing out flaws because I know what the bible says when it comes to pointing out the log in my brothers eyes:

So I know I should focus on my own flaws before I start pointing out others flaws, but it pains me to see Lost people especially believer who practice hate, who follow a man who lies to them as president and those choose to ignore the pain of others in need instead to practice what god hates.

I know we all fall short in this world and in the eyes of GOD, but we can all ask for forgiveness and we are forgiven on the shot, what a great GOD. If would only practice what we preach we would all be better people. I can't expect those who don't believe to practice not doing what god hates, but I see many non christians do which put many to shame.

What is the point of the message is NOT to point out what we shouldn't do, but really a message for myself to remember that I am not perfect, I too do things GOD hates and I need to stop. I am NOT holier than thou, but I am a man who strives to be better each day and some days I do take a step back but I move forward again. This

Blog may be more geared for believers but for who don't believe this may go to show you what GOD hates and how we can strive to be better.

Lastly I know that many may not like this Blog because NO likes to be told what GOD hates, because many will equate that with GOD being unloving but that is quite the opposite because GOD loves all of us regardless of what we think. GOD only wants the best for us and to rely on him for our needs when it can be difficult its easy to rely on ourselves, but I see seek him, Pray and see what happens God is faithful to us.

I know from reading this many will say hey your just a Trump hate, first and foremost I DONT hate anyone I Hate that we have a man as president who practices ALL the things GOD hates and yet Evangelicals are accepting of him. I have truly interacting with many online and although its a small percentage I speak to and I can not speak on behalf of all Christians and I choose NOT to, this is what I observe. Now If this is the direction our church is going into then we are in serious trouble. What will happen when Trump is NOT in office will the church recover from the years they practice to hate fellow man, to accept a man who they followed for years and destroyed the rule of law and republic. I am being over dramatic some of you will say I am, but I see what is happening around me and its scary.

Here is a scripture I truly see today taking place and although this scripture is true to any generation, day, year and time, it is even more true today. There are literally hundreds of scriptures if not thousands that talk about evil in the world and those practice it. I am not self righteous in understanding my faults I know I am flawed seriously, but each day I work on my relationship with Jesus to be a better man, husband, father, brother and son.

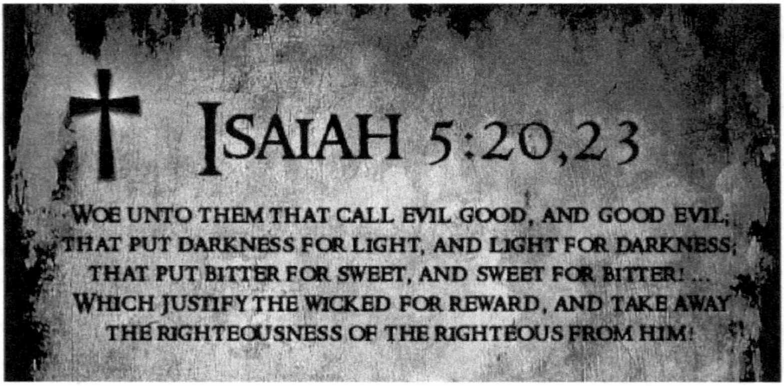

What has been so shocking to me that those I do speak with say I am lost, I am letting the devil working through me because I am making an attempt for others to open their eyes to deception like this this wolf in sheep's clothing.

Yes I am triggered each day and maybe I need to lay off the social media, I am NOT a news watcher but I see Twitter and Facebook have the same negative affect. I know social media is NOT reality but those are still people voices many negative who appear un-rational. Many will say I am being un-rational people have a right to believe what they want, what right do I have to tell people what to believe, but at the end of the day there is still right and wrong, truth and lies, what will you choose to believe, many will believe the lie without thinking, without investigation that is NOT me.

Thank you for taking the time to read this and know that is has been in my heart and mind for quite some time and it will continue to be on my mind and heart for years to come. I do believe that one day Christ will come back and take us to heaven it could today, tomorrow or a hundred years from now only GOD knows but in the mean time I am here and continue to search for the truth and not believe the lies of the Devil or what the world tells me to believe.

For those out there who are Christians I hope you see my heart and where I am coming from . Those who are Non-believers know my concerns come from what I see in our country taking place and refuse to bow down to a man who I see only cares for himself and only has an agenda to help himself be enriched for his own financial gain, something many followers of Trump have said I am wrong, and with everything I say there has been research, studies even to his mental fitness which I believe he is unfit to be president, but I respect the republic because people voted for him, hopefully a learned lesson to what can happen when we choose the wrong people.

I am open minded, I am intelligent in my assessment of what I believe, but wrong is wrong, never will wrong be just ok or right as long as Christian agenda is made. GOD is once again in control of what happens in our life although we all have a choice and thank GOD because many countries take away a persons right of choice and we are republic with freedoms that I see are at stake each day due to the corruption taking place in the office of presidency, congress , senate and our country, lets wake up!

Lastly be kind to each other , love one another and in the words of the great Fred Rogers:

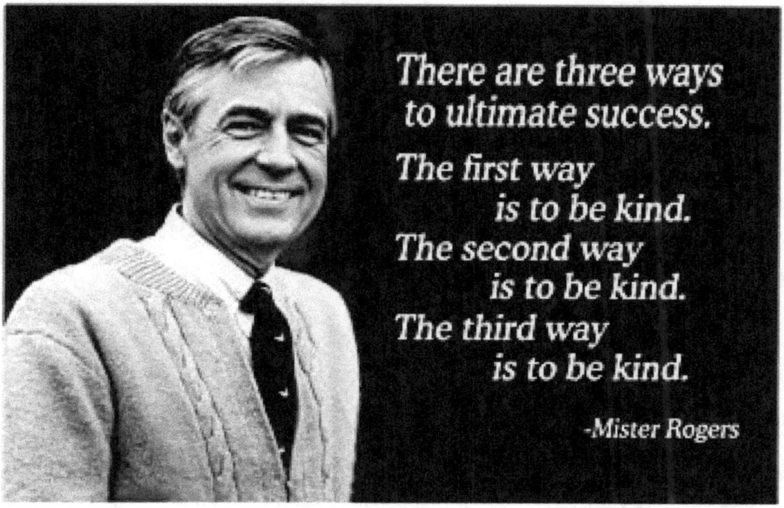

Thank you once again for taking the time to letting me unload my heart as this blog has been sitting in draft since May of 2019 and finally could no longer hold on to my feelings. Until we meet again!

Chapter 25

Choosing Leadership Without Morality

Original title: The Consequences of Choosing Leadership Without Morality

November 6, 2024

Today I am overcome with raw emotion, I am unsure why I am so affected by our countries political decisions, where its something that takes place every four years, like clockwork. This time is different though, as the country voted for a felon, an adulterer, a rapist, a cheat, a Liar and yet people are overjoyed to him in the office. I get it no person is perfect, only god is perfect, but God's people voted him office, despite his lack of morality and ethics, bringing hypocrisy front and center. Don't get me wrong

I am follower of Jesus, I believe Jesus and God are in control and God knew what was coming, it was per-ordained. I would love to think that #47 will bring peace to the country and unite men and women together, but I know that will not happen.

I guess the other side of the coin, is people can say well Biden and Harris are no better, especially during COVID, imposing their Work Ideology on LGBTQ , Abortion issues, shaping the countries to be more open to immorality, claiming they turned our country dark with a new belief system. I ask myself how has Democrats messaging and policies affect me and I can say they have not, but have when it comes to the cost of living making it affordably to live, Inflation and I dont believe Trump will do any better as he is someone who wishes only to help the rich, playing on idea that he believes in Christian values. But he cares for no one but himself, enriching himself and basically staying out of prison, not that would have ever happened, but good try.

I suspect he will do what he states he will do incorporate a form on concentration camps, add more judges, turn the courts even more conservative, remove rights from the people especially voting rights so that we will try to remove the ability to vote in future elections and just allow him to rule like Putin and other dictators. You may say you are being a fool to think that will happen, but when men and women allow democracy to fail, it will fail and we have no one to blame but ourselves.

The End Has Arrived!

Our time as a country is coming to an end and the reckoning is here as well as our punishment for how we as people turn our back on God, even through who proclaim to love Jesus. Although I don't know another man or women's heart, only God does, but evil continues and that is nothing new as it has only gotten more pronounced in society with men of influence and money to wield change to control the lives of people. We as a country love to point fingers at other countries for the control over their citizen like Iran, North Korea, Russia, Asia and eastern European countries, giving us a blue print for what can be done towards it citizens, removing rights and abilities to live a good life, that is what is on the way.

I know many may not agree, but what I see so men specifically wish to put down other men, especially men and women of color, immigrants, different sexual orientations and lifestyles that don't align with old world views, that men and women who are different don't belong in society and even those like myself who struggle with mental illness should be shipped away, place in some asylum because that is what man feels is best.

Going back in history

We are truly stepping back into history, repeating errors of the past, instead of progressing, we are going back. How is okay in today's world where its perfect acceptable to elect leaders who put down humans, remove rights and dictate those who choose to live their and cant believe government says its wrong, its immoral yet men and women in power are allowed to live their lives anyway they see fit.

Ideologies that many thought were forgotten and thought to be destructive to society are coming back in full force, because some man and women felt they know what is best for society. I get for any government there are ideologies and policies felt to improve society and have a better quality of life, but how does the future look for most of society.

Political parties on both sides have failed their constituents but at least with one party, we remain a democracy and the other we get closer and closer to dictatorship. Many will say we are not a dictatorship, never will be and your being dramatic and there are guardrails to protect us, but those guardrails have been tested over the years, seen to be weak and yes we have tried to strengthen those, but those policies and often laws were denied, because parties could see the advantages of keeping them in place.

The Test of Democracy AGAIN!

Now our democracy will be surely tested over the next four years, some of what is going to happen is going to damage our country for decades to come along with the effects over the citizens, bringing uncertainty to the people. I feel that uncertainty knowing that instability in a country only brings great stress, pain and many not getting the support they need. I truly believe today will affect many to the point of a lost hope in what we thought is people making the right decisions in who to bring into power.

I am saddened that we lived in such a stupid, immoral and unethical society putting aside a man's or womens threat to our world. As if we lived in Nazi Germany and the rise of power of Adoff Hitler whose rise mimics much like today and look how that turned out. Instead of the gas chambers, we will have concentration camps of immigrants and anyone who gets caught, shipped out, allowed to be abused, raped, and killed all in the name of saving the country from people who are not a threat to society, but what do I know. You would think after over centuries of what we have done in this country we would have learned.

I do know there is one group of people who surely have experienced great harm to this country are the native Americans/ indigenous people of our country who were displaced, killed, murdered and shipped off in far lands with their rights removed. You see not much as changed, as instead of doing this to native Americas today, we are going to do to other vulnerable groups of people who only wish to live in peace and take care of their families, but our message to you, is go somewhere else.

I truly believe there are overjoyed to see people shipped off imprisoned as being a land of opportunity and a land welcoming to world is no longer welcoming, as I often see life imitate art as I think of the film “Gangs of New York” and other films that are coming to our reality very soon.

God is in Control, but Still have Free Will for NOW

Again God is in control, these years will be a test and a punishment to much of society for wanting a king, something that is reminiscent of King Saul and look how that turned out, because in the end man and women are untelligent and ability to lead as God is the only one that knows how to lead with purpose, but even men and women who say they know God do not. I get it that when comes to political parties' democrats do not align to the values of a Christian as many of the policies and actions revolve around keeping abortion, trans right and bringing woke ideas into our culture, but at least at the end of the day we are not a dictatorship.

Democrats don't rule over me, tell me what I cant believe or try to shove religion down my throat, its my choice to decided what to believe where as the other party feels its there place to tell me what to believe, when we live in a world and country where we have choice, unlike countries like Iran where you can not be Christian or China, or North Korea and if found to be one, will be imprisoned and or killed, we are not better than those countries as we will truly take evil to new levels, but who cares right. If the rich get what they want everyone is happy, who cares for the peasants or shall we say citizens of the country.

I pray for my daughter's future in the coming years, luckily she's in middle school, the effects of what we do will be have long last effects in our society and the way we live, as the power is taken from the people and swifts to elites, thinking of the phrase "Let them eat cake" and we shall eat it for four long years, here's to the end of democracy as we know it. It was a nice ride.

I will say we were warned time and time again, but our history, but even by those who have written of what is to come if we allow certain people to rule over us and perils we will experience as we will be truly be in Orwellian era of 1984.

Chapter 26

The Battle for America: Disinformation

Original title: The Battle for America: Disinformation and Its Consequences

November 10, 2024

No, I will not let it go!

I don't why I am so bothered over the fact that Kamala Harris lost the presidency and that we now will have a president who has vowed destruction of the United States, something we saw first hand in his first presidency. Most of us may not have been truly affected, but maybe you were, as the years of 2016 – 2020, were quite horrid as these were not a time or prosperity but of pain inflicted on the innocent.

You see, I am partial to those people we call immigrants, migrants who come to this country undocumented or not, they are still human. The argument is by many, is they don't believe here, they need to go back to their own country and stop messing up the good ole Amerika as millions come here searching for the American dream, a dream in my opinion that is on its death bed.

These immigrants who do jobs that so many of use will not do, feeling as though we are above that line of work like jobs in agriculture, picking fruits and produce for the American people, or the person who cuts and landscapes our lawns and the lawns of America, most don't want to get paid those low wages.

We live in a culture where many find working in fast food too good, low skilled and for teenagers, but surprisingly many adults work in those industry propping up the fast-food nation, hardworking Americas, frankly it makes Americans seem downright lazy. I get it we are not lazy, but have grown accustomed to jobs in technology, easy money being influencers.

I truly believe people are under the illusion that the future president will care about the people, the common folk, the little guy, but his only concern is himself, enriching himself, empty words, lies. What angers me most of all is how Evangelicals Christians have fallen for his lies, his immorality, the hate that he spreads, like a virus.

Sadly, we as a country were duped by misinformation from the media and social media, using its reach to reach millions across the globe. I have no social media, no Tik

Tok, Face Book, X, but do have a Linkedin, which is becoming a mini- Facebook and eventually I will just stop going to a site dedicated to professionals and job searching.

Yes, there are bad actors out there, who wish to only caused harm to our country and our election systems, which only proves, we need more protections. Miraculously there was no fraud in our elections this year, but apparently there was much fraud in previous years and I am positive the coming years, our ability to Vote will be removed and leaders will just be placed and not voted for, where we can have a true dictatorships like in mother Russia.

Disinformation was foretold Decades ago

Disinformation has been weaponized and now can be used to change the truth, and make untruths facts. Where have I seen that before, oh yes by a man who I believe prophesied what can happen to society if we don't pay attention reading the works of "1984" and "Animal Farm".

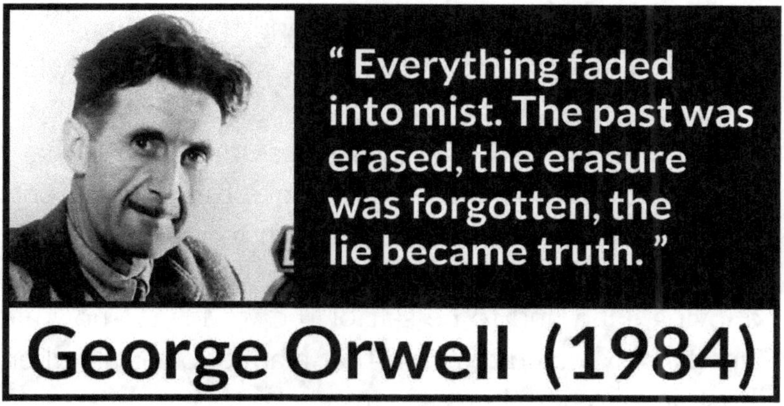

Jesus is my Savior Period

As a follower of Jesus myself, he stands for nothing, but what I see is fellow brethren, people of God see him as some type of savior against the people in this country and the world. Now one may say, well, you should be happy he president, he is going to make the country better, promote Christianity and allow people to say "Merry Christmas" again.

This is a man who hates, a man wants to destroy the different, those in the LGBTQ community, Latinos and people of color. I get it as a Christian, I am against abortion, but understand its not a cut and dry issue, women have choices to do what they want with their bodies, who am I say what they can and can not do.

If a woman decides to have an abortion, that is between her and God, not between her and the U.S. Government and in my opinion have no place. Yet we have a president who has already made it impossible for women to make choices with their bodies and that was only the beginning as we have four more years and beyond in whoever he decides to put in place.

I am angered that churches across the country have promoted him as a man who will make this country better, despite his fear mongering, his out for blood attitude, but that is not a big deal. We are taught a Christians to be loving, kind and to be salt of the world. Yet how are Christians expected to act in that manner be a salt when Christians promote him as being good.

The Double Standards from Christians

Never have the heard evangelicals question his morality or speak out against his ethics, still feeling the need to destroy the democrats, Joe Biden, Kamala as their voices have magnified from the right and Christian pastors like Greg Laurie, Franklin Graham and others who have prominent voices that reach millions of people as the voice of reason.

Maybe some may say I am not a real Christian, not a believer because I don't follow Mr. President into the deeps of hell and follow his lead, kiss the ring so to speak. I follow Jesus, what he says will happen and yes he prophesied that there will be men like Mr. President who exist and God allows them to exist not because they are ordained, but because GOD has a plan for America and its not necessary a plan that is meant to heal the nation, but also to punish the people for their sins. Yes we all sin in this world, including myself, everyone of us is not immune to God's punishment and his is coming to America, I believe and we all must suffer as a country because we learn our lessons.

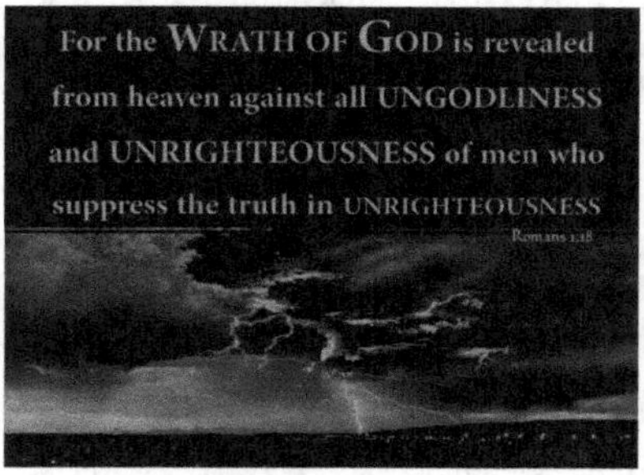

In my opinion this sums up what America is. Don't get me wrong America was founded on Judaeo Christian principles, but we have far strayed from those principles. Due to our greed and our prosperity in this nation, it must come to an end eventually and that time appears to be approaching.

<u>This Shall Pass too, but at what Cost</u>

Some would say well it's only four years, it will go fast, stop worrying, it will be okay, NO IT WILL NOT. This future president doesn't want to be called a fascist or a dictator but that is what he is and or will become because he will be enabled to as even the Supreme court said so. Now I get it most did not know Kamala, only from her record as a prosecutor, a California AG, Senator and Vice President, experience and happens to be a woman. A woman who I believe has the ability to govern, but that is not what the people wanted. Its like going to the doctor and needing a surgeon but decide to go to Tijuana and have our surgery in a back alley because its cheaper, no offense to Tijuana, Mexico.

Personally I didn't care about Kamala, I didn't know her or know her personally, but only what she stood for in the sense of justice. She is democrat, fights for the progressives, something that I know the Right hates and even Christians, because it goes against the moral fabric of who we are, as we are promoting abortion, LGBQT lifestyles and immorality, but the reality is we are all human who has free will and choice to live our lives as we see fit, something GOD ordained from the beginning. In the end, we either go to heaven or hell, but as a Christians we are told to be lights to those who we don't align with, but to love always, be true representatives of Jesus, I cant truly say that the Christians of today, especially the Presidents followers.

I truly believe there is too much focus on the lifestyles of people in general, frankly who cares what orientation a person is, let people live their lives as they see fit, how are they harming me, how are they paying my bills, how do those people affect my life. Yes I understand the culture changes, beliefs change and we are fools to think we can remain in the 1950's, not going to happen. What we must do is teach ourselves and families to be more loving, accepting of others and focus on our own lives, yet Democrats and Republicans are so wrapped up into what people do in bed, behind closed doors, that is business that is between the person and God. We have people who act as moral police who are immoral themselves yet we let them dictate policies and laws on others.

Celebrities did this Election NO GOOD!

There is one other part of elections especially that didnt help, celebrity endorsements, mean nothing! A celebrity has no more influence than the common man and women and why would a person take the word of Taylor Swift or George Loonie or Oprah or Cardi B, their voices although influential have no influence as most of us think of as just entertainers, but that did hurt this election.

I truly don't believe many of those artist truly believe in democracy or the democrats as they have their millions of dollars and fans, what more do they need in this world as there are those who are struggling with poverty, homelessness and far worse problems they will and can never imagine. Seriously what does Taylor Swift know of poverty as the world as embraced her, coveted her and made her a very wealthy women with great power. I get she is talented I am not taking that away from her, but at the end of the day has no real power to make change in the country and why should she, she is an entertainer.

As a country we have bigger problems, and this election only proved that we as a country cannot appreciate nor wanted a woman as president and a woman of color to lead our country. I get that we got Obama for eight years and wanted to go back to our roots of a White male president, which we have had for most presidents.

As a Christian Man, I know whatever happens its in God's control, especially where our country is going and who is leading, but they are not Godly men and women, despite what the media wants us to believe, loyalist to the President only to do his bidding only to cause harm to the people and destroy from within.

I understand I may sound nuts and sound like some conspiracy nut but I believe in looking back to our past and the repeat of the past into the future, which is upon us, especially if you look to the history and rise of Adolf Hitler, mimicking America today. George Santayana, couldn't have said it wiser, "Those who cannot remember the past are condemned to repeat it,"

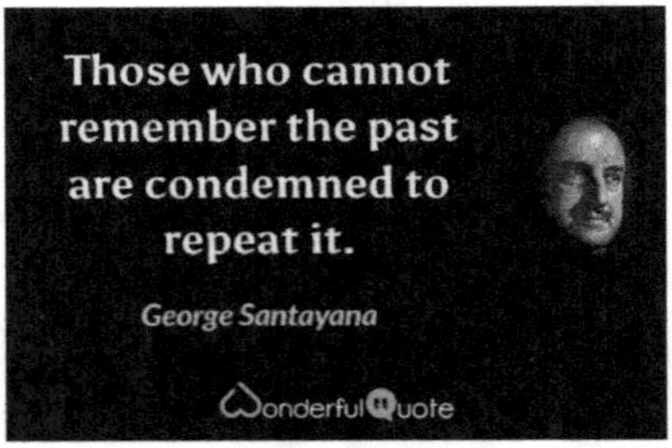

As a country that prides itself on being highly intelligent and evolved, we are so stupid to the obvious all in the pursuit and wealth and power, forgetting the prime example of Rome, which fell in the same way America is. Unfortunately, we choose not to listen or remember history.

I pray my anger subsides, as I need to turn to my bible more in these times! Pray for me and truly for America, but yes as hard as it is to say, Pray for Trump to truly come to Jesus, but my mind I doubt he will ever come to Jesus, yet as Christians we can only hope.

I will not get over my feelings for some time and I am aware that will not change anything as what is done is done, God has allowed what will happen to take place, May God Help us. I know as a country we have major issues, one of them is our own citizens and those who need help like the homeless and those who struggle with mental illness, but there are humans who come to this country for help, failed by their own country, why should he harm them in the process, losing our humanity. Treat everyone with respect and kindness and who cares where they came from, they are not our concern, they are the concern of God's, he will care for them.

On a positive note, Yes the future is what you make and if one of the greatest film series Back to the future have taught us, the future can change from the choices we make today, we have choice over our futures, so lets make a good one.

Chapter 27

Lessons Not Learned: History's Warning for America

November 18, 2024

I have great confliction over where this country is going as I feel I am on the other side of that part of time that lives deep in me, my faith and my belief in Jesus. As a Christian, It pains me to see citizens of this country fall in line to a president who they proclaim will make America great again. How did we fall for this bullshit of messaging that our president is the savior of the world omitting Jesus Christ the true savior but yet it angers me to see pastors and so call Christians preach to the high heaven of their Love for President elect, as I cannot even say his name.

Many may say, I have a problem, what is my problem is we will have a 34-time convicted felon as our president, a swindler, a rapist, unethical, immoral man. I get it some may say, well no one is perfect. The last time I check, I have never raped anyone, embezzled or cheat but I get it because he used the law to get what he wanted along with his wealth and name and be able to state the law and get away with it even today. Any other person who have been in prison a long time ago, but not him, he is the golden king of the United States.

I guess what angers me is when I see prominent pastors like Greg Laurie, Franklin Graham and other preach about the goodness of the man, never, ever saying anything against the man, but sure the current president is the problem, he is the one taking our freedoms away, he is the one who is trying to wipe religious freedom from us and make us a woke nation.

As a nation, progressive views and equality are nothing new as we have learned from the histories of the world on the dangers of following the ideology of things like eugenics, white supremacy and keeping racism alive in America, when we should have learned a long time ago the dangers men and women can inflict on a society by having dangerous views like Adolf Hitler.

People forget what this man truly did, being that seems like ancient history, but its not, as Nazi Germany is here again, except we may not have gas chambers yet, but will have encampments on the way, mass deportations, the rise and hate and next the real purge of America. The world is in shock of the United States, being once the leader in humanity, but no more, forgetting our heritage that we are both an immigrant nation and a Christian nation, but lets be clear our land was founded by the native Americas or indigenous people who we kicked off their land as many today still forget the savageness of what was done to them and even today what is done to them. Just because they have their land, their small slice means nothing as all of the lands were there and they cared for the land, but we as Americans have spoiled the lands, rotting it to what it has become, and we continue to do so today.

Has History Taught Us Nothing

We have not learned from history, we have only gotten worse and continue to spread hate to those who are different, who choose to live differently than others. What amazes me today, is even as a Christian, you hear and feel the hate from other Christians who preach goodness and about the wicked pointing out the LGBTQ community, their sinfulness about how they will go to hell, how unworthy they are. This message is not from GOD, as God loves the world and wants no one to go to Hell.

Wickedness has been going on since Adam and Eve and will not cease until Jesus comes back, but we have an opportunity to repent and turn to Jesus. Believe it or not have had friends, co-workers, colleagues who are not born again, who gay, lesbian and apart of the LGBQT community, do I hate them, wish harm to them, NO! They are just trying to live, survive like anyone else, but the message from many prominent churches is you are not wanted. The damage this does to so many people as those Christians are not true witnesses to the Love of Jesus, how do we expect those unsaved to learn and turn their hearts to Jesus, when all they get is hate and damnation.

Sadly people are giddy with excitement as I was watching a recent service of Pastor Greg Laurie, who was jumping with joy over the President elect getting re-elected and how he was going to change things for the better. That we should pray for him to come to Jesus and in a way saying he was a good man, saved by God when he didn't die by assignation. Comparing him to President Reagon and his own assignation.

The president elect is nothing like President Reagan and I am sure he is turning over in his grave at the sight of what America has become, but yes go ahead compare him. Mind you I was born in 1979, so he was president when I was only a baby, I truly don't know what he was like, only what I have read and seen on the television.

I do believe he was a good man and president, but like any president changed the course of history for the rest of us even today. The republicans today are also nothing like Reagan but what he started has led us here. Now there is nothing wrong with conservative values, but today's republicans are no conservatives and go against what Republicans like Reagan fought for.

Our Judgment has arrived!

I will say God is in control, has always been and will always be as what is happening in America was going to happen, but I know for most we are surprised over the turn of events, which is not news to GOD. I believe yes God spared president elect but not for the reasons many think, as he could simply use men and women, not to bring peace and prosperity but allow a man and women to teach the nation a lesson which in essence is like spanking from God, as we as nation have turned away from goodness, we have become fat and greedy, hateful, immoral and unethical people , which deserves judgment, are you ready, but judgment is coming, something we all deserve like any good father and this has been a long time coming, May God Bless America and what is to follow in the next four years and beyond.

Chapter 28

Future Fears: Power, Corruption, Decline

Original title: Future Fears: Power, Corruption, and Society's Decline

November 23, 2024

The fear of the unknown is real, especially the future of U.S. and I get that I may be over dramatic in thinking the worst is upon us, but for many I don't know if they see the true significance of what is happening. For many the political process is normal as we elect a new president, but believe it or not our democracy is still new as we are not thousands of years old, but a few hundred years which is not a long time.

The Fall of America, like Rome

We have come to a crossroads when yes its possible that our democracy could end, because frankly without the guidance and advisement of moral and ethical people that its not possible as people will push the limits to get what they want whether its power or money or both. We live in an age where money can buy you anything influence, riches and anything one desires.

We truly live in a deprived world of sin, lust and greed and its only gets worse as people follow others, act as they act with no consequences. For example, If I wanted to do harm to someone, I could potentially be allowed. But many would say no you can not do what you want, you would go to prison, the Law would step in. Well, why doesn't the law step in for the rich in sense of accountability and consequences.

Two Systems of Government

There are two systems of governance in the United States, one for the rich and the other for poor so to speak. I guess I fall into the poor category, where if I was to embezzle, murder, cheat and steal, I would surely go to prison. People who are in positions of power like government, no harms rarely come to them.

I often struggle with whats the point, what is standing between me and anarchy to acting out my angry and taking it out on the world like others do, being a real A-hole to the world, despite the fact I consider myself a Christian and believer in GOD, which would make me a hypocrite. So many men and women in this world do cause harm, doing despicable horrible things like murder, debauchery, treating fellow men, women and child like a piece of property as we go back to a time when humans were nothing but a slave. Although human slavery man not exist in the U.S. it still does exist to a degree in other countries as many would think we as people have evolved, but we have not evolved, we've only gotten worse.

The Great Conflict

I guess the greatest conflict I see is men and women who say they stand for JESUS yet do horrible deeds to each other. We live in country of so-called freedoms such as freedom of religion and speech but is it really free. Although I have the ability to write , blog, Podcast and VLOG to put my thoughts out there, there could be consequences to my thoughts and beliefs as people have the ability to take my words and use them against me especially in cases if I was to say derogatory things about people, spread hate, yet people do it every day, especially who also preach the name of Jesus about their hate for LGBQT people, migrants and immigrants and how they are drain on society, how they loath and dislike them calling them horrible names as if they were subhuman, that is NOT JESUS. Yet we are free for the most part to say what we like, spreading hate like wildfire, using the means of social media to catch fire across the world to millions and even billions of people each day.

The other disappointment is people fall hook, line and sinker for the lies from those who are supposed to speak truth, even from a preacher. I see that and yet I try not to judge but these are men who are supposed to be highly moral and ethical, but yet they say things that tells the world I really do hate you. I don't have people, like most we have bias, we may stereotype which I know I need to correct because words, values and beliefs are embedded in our skin its difficult to remove them. I am not perfect nor will ever claim to but know that I too have the tendency to judge prematurely.

Decline of Morality in Faith Leaders

But as look around, men and women who we as society respect are no longer respectful. Frankly I know they don't care, they get what they need out of society, whether its money, power and influence. I am thinking of Pastor Greg Laurie and Franklin Graham, two preachers who are in fact friends and who both have great influence. I am not saying they are immoral or unethical, frankly I don't know but they preach highly of the president elect and former president as being a man of valor, a man who will save our crumbling decrypted society from ruin and to bring Jesus back to the table. Jesus never left, he has always been here, its Society who has rejected Jesus and people have only gotten worse over the years in turning their backs on the Jesus, but Jesus still loves them and US.

The loss of Hope

Men, women and children are losing hope in this world as men and women continue to show us how easy it is to take advantage making others feel powerless. I do ask myself often what the point is of living in this world, why must I live in a world where men and women care nothing for each other, only wish to do harm to each other, where is the love.

Apart of the problem, we many no longer live, living in a cyber world of disconnection, no real human connection and contact, where it feels due to that reason, why must we continue being a society of rules, laws and civility when others live in a world where civility doesn't exist, again treating each other like disposable garbage.

As believer, we are to follow Jesus and not man, but a preacher is a man, who in today's culture uses the pulpit to preach about president elects and how great they are and how are country will be so much better for society, but I don't see it that way. I do see society crumbling in despair, getting worse due to moral depravity, lack of ethics and concern for human kind .

The next four years will a lot about the horrors that men and women are capable of as people in power project lawlessness, fear, hate, anger towards their own citizens as they stand behind that they are doing everything for the people to help them, but that is lie. The people in power take pleasure in hurting others, murdering them and if history shows us anything we will be in the history books and not in a good way, another form of Nazi, Germany, but instead we will treat immigrants, people of color and our citizens as human garbage as people will be executed, placed in cages for in cages for years and children will grow up seeing that hate is okay.

It pains me to write this and some again may think that what the media says will never happen, we have laws and guardrails in place to protect our society. If anything we may even have our version of the purge , a legal way to kill people and whittle down our society. Again this four years will tell but will say we will all be changed and not for the better, as our society is so stupid after all, supposed to be highly intelligent beings but failed that test, we ultimately deserve what is coming our way.

Buckle people, we are in for a real ride!

Part III – Bigfoot, Monsters and Film

Chapter 29

In Honor of Apollo Creed – RIP

February 4, 2024

Where would Rocky Balboa be with out Apollo Creed. The actor who played Apollo Carl Weathers passed peacefully on February 1st, 2024. A accomplished actor, athlete and director.

As a Rocky loved , I can not imagine Rocky without Carl Weathers playing Apollo as he was meant for that role. In actuality when Sly Stallone made Rocky, Carl was the star and Sly an unknown.

What is quite sad and understandable is that those actors who were in the original Rocky films, 1-5 are pretty much almost gone, except of course Sly and Talia (Adriannn!!) and Dolph Lundgren The last death prior to Carl was Burt Young who passed October 8th, 2023. Obliviously each person will eventually pass, who knows when but when Sly passes that will be particularly difficult for me.

As a Rocky loved , I can not imagine Rocky without Carl Weathers playing Apollo as he was meant for that role. In actuality when Sly Stallone made Rocky, Carl was the star and Sly an unknown.

What is quite sad and understandable is that those actors who were in the original Rocky films, 1-5 are pretty much almost gone, except of course Sly and Talia (Adriannn!!) and Dolph Lundgren The last death prior to Carl was Burt Young who passed October 8th, 2023. Obliviously each person will eventually pass, who knows when but when Sly passes that will be particularly difficult for me.

RIP Carl Weathers, (AKA Apollo Creed) and Burt Young (Pauley).

Chapter 30

Exploring the Dark Legacy of Candyman

October 20, 2024

As we are now in October, let the horror fests begin as films start creeping into each of the streaming services, most of my favorites from Nightmare on Elm Street, Halloween's (Except the Rob Zombie) versions, Exorcist and Exorcist III and many others.

One that I found great interest in as far the story is Candy Man, another favorite having watched all the versions and of course I will throw in all the Saw's, Insidious and the list goes on with too many too count forgive me if I do not mention your favorite.

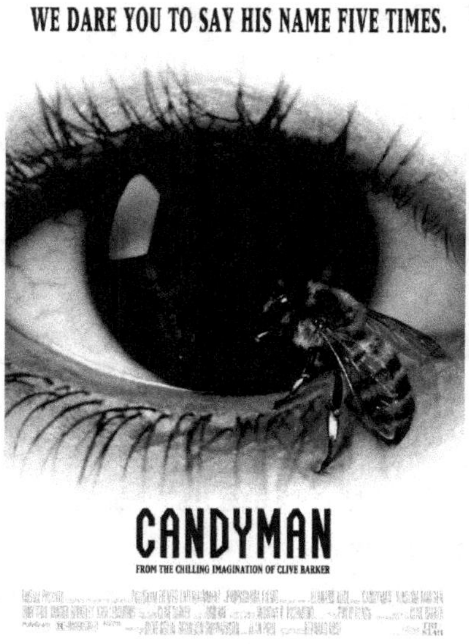

But Candy Man, having watched the original film when I was about twenty years old and didn't really see two and three until years ago and then of course the most recent adaptation.

I find that many will consider Candy Man the villain as yes, he kills people who say his name five times. CANDY MAN, CANDY MAN, CANDY MAN, CANDY MAN, CAN- , sorry I can not do it frankly I don't want to meet my maker with the Candy Man.

What I find interesting about his story is it is a story of Love ending in violence. First, I love how this story was written by Clive Barker with his short story "The Forbidden". Having not read the original story but feel I must read.

As the original story was actually a Caucasian male having long blonde hair with an unruly red beard, Pale skin that is yellow and eyes that looked like rubies. I find this version quite frightful. In the film version he is played by the incredible Tony Todd, who is black but plays an incredible Candyman less.

Granville T Candyman or Daniel Robitaille was a part of a rich black family in 1870's Chicago. Having gained fame for his portraits and music he commissioned to paint Helen, the daughter of a wealthy landowner. Demanding that Helen poses in the nude as Venus and soon their relationship turns to love.

The forbidden affair brings the city's wrath down to Granville. Cutting his right painting hand off with a rusty blade, covering his naked body with Honey and watching as the bees sting him to death. Lastly the lynch mob chants Candyman five times before he dies. In the short story, the character describes his existence as an urban legend: "I am rumor. It's a blessed condition, believe me. To live in people's dreams; to be whispered at street-corners; but not have to be."

The story revolves around the needs to keep the legacy alive, killing those who doubt his existence. Based on the legend, Candy man was wrong, seeking his revenge through the ages, keeping his legacy alive. Did the town need to lynch the man, cut his hand off, insert a hook, cover with honey, and let bees sting him to death. Some would say just move on, don't take your revenge, revenge is wrong. It's hard because as a man who believes in GOD,

I know GOD say's vengeance is his and it is, but when will people just learn probably never. Even today people continue to take their vengeance, harm the innocent and yet at times there seems to be no accountability.

What is interesting is there are other films that despite ideas about those who do harm getting what we think they deserve like SAW or Jigsaw who attempted to teach those who wrong others to learn and seek repentance for their acts.

I wonder do we need more Candyman's in the world, more Jigsaws, hard to say because then maybe one day we might be on the other end paying for our crimes, our sins. Again, a follower of Christ my sins are forgiven that doesn't mean we don't pay for them in some way.

I do feel bad for the Candyman at times, because why can't people just let people be, mind their own business, but again even today people continue to act terrible towards their fellow man, woman and even child.

I think there are certainly lessons we can learn from some of these films, although I do not people to die, I do wish people to learn to be kinder to each other, stop the hate, the violence, the smearing , the bullying but I doubt that will ever happen because frankly we live in a fallen , rotten world that will not be changed until Christ comes back.

Like any story, idea there is a lesson behind it, a lesson the writer is trying to teach their audience that we often overlook, but Candy Man I think has a clear message, but I may be mistaken.

I would encourage you all to watch and even read about the Candyman who knows what this story may tell you about yourself, your views.

Chapter 31

Rediscovering Halloween Traditions Through Family

October 20, 2024

Happy Halloween everyone to those who celebrate and to those who don't. Strangely I am someone who doesn't really celebrate this day and its not completely because of my faith. You see growing up I was like most children and even young adults who celebrated by dressing up, going trick or treating and handing out candy. I loved to decorate the home for Halloween which included fake spider webs and a realistic dummy I would hang from our tree in the front yard.

Growing up with all the classic horror films Halloween, Nightmare on Elm Street, Child's play, Hellraiser and

Gremlins (Yes this is a horror film) and many others and I can not forget IT.

Movies always being my escape into another reality from my own life as its amazing that I remember more about seeing movies then about my own childhood.

During those years I dressed up, I was a few different characters including Freddy Kreuger, Michael Myers, E.T., Michelangelo the Teenage mutant ninja Turtle, Jason and I was a killer clown, Gizmo from Gremlins and I believe I was He-Man.

As a Christian we are taught not to celebrate this evil holiday as it's a day that gives honor to Satan and what it stands for. A time when Satanist worship their god and in pagan times would sacrifice babies on in honor of Baal. I personally don't just celebrate it for that but maybe Its difficult to fully separate myself from this day because I have a daughter who is eight years old. She personally has never had any real interest in this day herself and that could be because she doesn't see mom and dad celebrate it which is fine. We still want to give her a choice and in years she has said she didn't wish to dress up but loves when she is given candy.

One of my fondest memories of Halloween is that mom would take myself and sister to McDonalds on this day and get us our Happy meals that came with our plastic candy pail coming in a variety of colors and faces.

Mom always made a point to get us out of our own house of hell from the devil in carnet that we live with our grandfather. I guess there was no point in celebrating Halloween because we were living in a hellish situation at times. There were also times when we would spend this day with our father when we would spend time at grandma and grandpas and technically his home too pigging out on Pizza, soda, and candy watching scary movies and playing Nintendo for the whole weekend.

I guess you could say I had a someone average childhood despite parents being divorced we didn't miss out on holidays and those things a child should experience but it was still a sad time for myself as I always had to return back to the hell house.

Halloween does get me excited about what is to come in the coming weeks, one of favorite holidays Thanksgiving.

For those who celebrate today, dress up, hand out candy or just have a relaxing time at home remember these days even if they may seem not very important as I truly to think back on these days in my own childhood, looking at my daughter as she grows up so fast, I want her to remember these days.

Happy Halloween everyone, be safe, wear a mask and if you have a spooky mask where another one, LOL.

Chapter 32

The Legend of Krampus: A Different Christmas Story

December 22, 2024

Happy Krampusnacht or if you celebrate the feast of St. Nicholas.

Christmas time is here! Oh Christmas time, Oh Christmas time. For many and much of the world I know it can be hard to celebrate and why should we with Covid-19, Lock downs, high unemployment, people on the verge of losing everything. One could say Joseph where are your priorities, Christmas should be canceled this year.

I say hold on now, let's not get crazy and remember the reason for season which is Not only the celebration of Jesus our savior but of kindness, generosity towards one another. We are certainty in difficult times, and this will NOT be the last time society and the world suffers at the hands of a health crisis, but we must try to remain positive. I know this year will not be the same, but in hopes that next year will be better.

I particularly like Christmas and I do not at the same time. I like Christmas in the sense of the traditions that we celebrate with the people we love. I don't particularly like how Christmas is one big, commercialized time of the year to stick to the man or women to spend spend spend. Now some of you may say well you don't have to spend money if you don't want to and although that may be true, its usually a requirement in the United States. I mean how many of us like to receive but when it comes to giving back we decide to close our purse, it doesn't feel great.

The other reason is for many years growing up, frankly I can not remember one good Christmas, it seems like one big fog. I do remember those times being very sad and happy as my mother would cook delicious food, there would be presents, but there was always the presents of the Devil (my grandfather) who made the holiday's unbearable at times.

The Reason for the Season

As a Christian I do know the meaning of the season and I must remember that, but I also like to kind of the sillier things in Christmas like Santa, Elves, Magic, the north pole and all my love for Christmas movies and music.

But one of the figures in Christmas I am quite interested in is Krampus. Having grew up with Santa from a young age, obliviously I would like to believe he is real and in a way he is. Santa or Saint Nicolas was a real figure a 4th century Greek Christian bishop of Myra. Famous for his generous gifts to the poor, in particular presenting three impoverished daughters of pious Christian with dowries so that they would not have to become prostitutes.

He was very religious from an early age and devoted his life entirely to Christianity. Saint Nicolas legend carried on into many different forms throughout the ages from Father Christmas, Sinterklaas and many other well-known names depending on global origin. Being in the United States, British and Dutch versions of the gift giver merged further, eventually becoming Americanized into "Santa Claus".

I believe most of us know the history of Santa Claus, but how many know the history of Krampus, other than seeing the movie which added to my interest in this mythical figures or figures. Like anything else Santa is a gift giver while Krampus is a gift taker among other things.

Who is Krampus?

Krampus a central European folklore is a horned, anthropomorphic figure described as "Half-goat, half-demon" who during the Christmas season, punishes children who have misbehaved. This contrasts with Saint Nicholas for oblivious reasons.

The history of the Krampus figure has been theorized as stretching back to Pre-Christian Alpine traditions. It is said that the myth of Krampus was the son of Hel, Norse goddess of the underworld.

Although Krampus appears in various variations, most share some common physical characteristics. He is hairy, usually black or brown, has cloven hooves and horns of a goat. His long, pointed tongue lolls out and he has fangs.

Krampus carries chains, thought to symbolize the binding of the Devil by the Christian Church. He thrashes the chains for dramatic effect. The chains are sometimes accompanied with bells of various sizes. Of more pagan origins are the Ruten, bundles of birch branches that Krampus carries and with he occasionally swats children. Sometimes Krampus appears with a sack of a basket strapped to his back; this is to cart off evil children for drowning, eating or to transport to hell.

Krampusnacht, European and American Traditions

The feast of St. Nicholas is celebrated in parts of Europe on December 6th. On the preceding evening December 5th, Krampus night is when the wicked hairy devil appears on the streets. While Krampus is responsible for the bad. Nicholas dispenses gifts, while Krampus supplies coal and Ruten bundles.

Milk and Cookies for Santa but what do you give Krampus, well Schnapps of course, a strong distilled fruit brandy.

Europeans have been exchanging greeting cards feature Krampus since the 1800's. Sometimes introduced with Greetings from Krampus, the cards usually humorous rhymes and poems. Krampus is often featured menacingly over children. He is also shown as having one human foot and one cloven hoof. In some Krampus sexual overtones; he is pictured pursuing buxom women. Over time, the representation of Krampus in the cards have changed; older versions have a more frightening Krampus, while modern versions are cuter, more Cupid-like creatures.

In American it's quite the opposite with a picture of Fat jolly Santa eat cookies, with his reindeer, elves living in the north pole, so many different variations. In addition to Santa, cards typically have imagines of Jesus birth, three wise man, Star of Bethlehem in addition to a winter theme. Suffice to say you will never see Santa leering at Kids or buxom women as we have to remember that Santa originated with Christian principles.

As you can see the two difference between the two figures, obliviously there is so much more on Santa and his origins. Krampus is a folklore which wouldn't physically exist, but in sense if you believe in the devil like I do then its perfectly possible that Krampus could exist but I think I probably would have met him by now since all little boys and girls are good.

Krampus in Popular Culture

Reflecting on the 2015 Krampus film which ignited this blog and because it's the Christmas season of course, this film perfectly personifies rotten kids and family who are ungrateful with Max who wrote his letter to Santa but his cousins, aunt and uncle ruin the Christmas season, thinking to myself, Thank God I don't have a family like this. The film itself perfectly creates Krampus, the elves and creature alike in such a perfect way. I think personally we need to have more visits by Krampus in our world to teach people to be more grateful for what they have in this life especially today, where ungratefulness is at an all time high.

Watching the film and learning about Krampus I can't help but to think what kind of bad kids would lead Krampus to eat the children , drown them or transport them to hell and in reality if you think about it the Devil truly does wish to take anyone down man , women and child by whatever means to take us to Hell. Interesting how St. Nick and Krampus both appear to have some form of Christian roots especially dealing with Hell and a demon who wants to punish and take.

As a society we are supposed to learn our lesson how to be for giving and selflessness but truly do we ever get to that point, appearing that much of society is rotten to the core at times, I will not say everyone and really I have no idea what the true difference between the U.S. and lets the UK or China, but I would say that wealthy nations do have the propensity for much more greed than lets say other countries whose society may have less, but that is just a theory of course. The reality is anyone rich or poor can truly be ungrateful even for the breath we have each day.

Krampus is still celebrated today in traditional parades known as the Krampuslauf, where young men dressed as Krampus parade through the streets, scaring spectators and sometimes chasing them, although the tradition has been arguably appropriated for celebration.

What I find so beautiful is our beliefs in the United States versus those who live in Europe and have a different belief system involving both St. Nick and Krampus and wonder why do we find Krampus no so menacing here, almost like a joke, but I truly feel if Krampus entered the good ole U.S. there surely would be much better behaved kids and families appreciating what and who is in their life.

Have a fantastic Weekend and thank you for always going on these strange journeys with me and my fascination with strange which typically involves some type of horror movie that I get my influence. More to come as we kick off December and on to Christmas and the New Year!

Chapter 33

The Legacy of Groundhog Day

Original title: The Legacy of Groundhog Day: Film and Tradition Combined

February 2, 2025

Many may not notice or care but today is Grounds Hog day on February 2nd. A tradition derived from Pennsylvania Dutch observed regionally of a superstition that the groundhog emerges from his burrow if it sees its shadow, it will retreat back into its den and winter will go on for 6 more weeks and if it doesn't see its shadow spring will arrive early. In 2025, the shadow was seen, auguring six more weeks of winter

I find this tradition wholesome and fun and although I live in California we don't have any such tradition, but would truly love to take part in such a tradition, I am sure its a fun event to attend.

For those who don't know what a ground hog is, per Wikipedia :

The groundhog plays an important role maintaining healthy soil in woodlands and plains; as such, the species is considered a crucial habitat engineer. The groundhog is an extremely intelligent animal, forming complex social networks and kinship with its young; it is capable of understanding social behavior, communicating threats through whistling, and working cooperatively to accomplish tasks such as burrowing.

This day also has more of different meaning to myself as this also the name of a long time favorite film of mine, Groundhogs Day with Bill Murray (1993). A favorite I have been watching for decades, remembering when we saw in the theaters 32 years ago, when I was only 13 years old.

A favorite by many and hard to believe that Bill Murray was only 42 years old when this film came out, although as I have gotten older, found some of the film not appropriate for someone who was 13 at the time, and especially the person I am today, who remembers and has watched time and time again, all of the times Phil Connor committed suicide in so many different way.

The film is classic even today, as I remember when it came out on VHS we would continue to watch it over and over again, never getting tired of it, even today. If you haven't already I encourage to watch this film and learn a little about this favorite event.

Chapter 34

How Scrooge Teaches us Valuable Lessons on Kindnes

Original title: Merry Christmas! How Scrooge Teaches us Valuable Lessons on Kindness and Love

December 24, 2024

Merry Christmas to all!

Thank you so much for all of those who take the time to read my blog and are part of my life I truly do Love you all. I know this year has been particularly difficult with COVID, politics and the incredible times we are facing.

This year I have tried to be incredibly real with all of you concerning my thoughts, feelings and what is going on in my world as like any human I work to grow. For many who read my blogs you may or may not believe in my positions whether its in politics, my thoughts on societal changes taking place or just in general, but I try to be genuine and true to all.

Over time my views do and will change because I am constantly looking to change in a good way, something I encourage all of us to try to do. All to often people get stuck in one position in life and stay there unwilling to grow. I am not staying change or principles or values but we should all try to have an option mind and the acceptance of other thoughts and opinions something I think in today's society we greatly lack.

During this time of year its especially important to look at what is important, having watched Charles Dickens a Christmas Carol, a story that all too often we all take for granted as just being a film or book we can watch or read at Christmas, but the message can be appreciate all days in our life. We truly live in a time of greed and oppression of people, some of you out there may feel like there is no such thing in society and I would ask you to look deeper in those who are suffering today.

Ebenezer Scrooge a man of business who started out in a life of solitude and loneliness never truly felt loved hence the reason I think he rejected Love and stuck to the cold hard world of money and prestige. The story is so important to look at what happens when it set aside people in our life and focus on wealth instead of what is important. I get that we all need to live a life, we all need to eat, we all need to survive and most all want to prosper in life, but its tough.

Not everyone is born with a silver spoon in their mouth, many have to slowly work their way in life to create a life. Some in this life have incredible fortune in their life, lots of money, big house, nice care, supportive family and support system to make sure they succeed. While others struggle to make it, pinching pennies with little or no support system alone in this dark cold world failing to succeed in a world that says you are not good enough unless you have this or do this, I have lived this life. Yes I have my wife and daughter, my sister, father, brother in law who support me, but deep within side me I ask for more.

Back to Scrooge, a man who was in the perfect position to live a comfortable life in his wealth and not worry about where his next meal would come from or where he would live. While others were truly suffering like today. Interesting how Scrooge mentioned workhouses and prisons which he fully supported. Obliviously we know what prisons are , but workhouses or poor houses existed which where placed that supported those who could not survive on their own. Imagine if you will these were the places people went to work, not that there was anything wrong with that, but these were considered dismal horrible places eventually turning to place to care for the elderly and resembling almost a prison environment, but again maybe it could be better then being homeless. Remembering when Scrooge was approached for a donation telling those :

> "At this festive season of the year, Mr Scrooge, ... it is more than usually desirable that we should make some slight provision for the Poor and destitute, who suffer greatly at the present time. Many thousands are in want of common necessaries; hundreds of thousands are in want of common comforts, sir."
> "Are there no prisons?"
> "Plenty of prisons..."
> "And the Union workhouses." demanded Scrooge. "Are they still in operation?"
> "Both very busy, sir..."
> "Those who are badly off must go there."
> "Many can't go there; and many would rather die."
> "If they would rather die," said Scrooge, "they had better do it, and decrease the surplus population."

The coldness in his voice, the heartlessness so reminiscent of today and the coldness in people today. I will say that I know that's Not everyone, many do care for sick and unfortunate like the homeless but there is very little help compared to the size of our societies today, we need more. It's so oblivious when you've made it life why should you have to give back, thinking only what how no one helped you succeed but in reality, you were helped,

GOD provided for you, giving you the mind and body, you have to today along with the gifts in your life something many forget. But again, Scrooge eventually say that through the three ghosts of Christmas Past, Present and Future.

I love that Dickens focused on this in his book because its something we should all see in hopes of redeeming ourselves and our souls to be better. Now you may think well I am good person and maybe you are but you can always be better.

Scrooge was redeemed by seeing his life from his past, but the biggest impacts were the present and future being able to see his impact on Bob Crachit , his family and Tiny Tim forgetting the impact people make in those lives we touch whether we think so or not. Ultimately Scrooge was even able to see his own death in a way and those people who truly despised and hated him, something again we should all see because many live-in illusions we are well loved, and we are not.

The ending is by far the best part of this incredible story as Scrooge corrects his ways immediately. He doesn't say well maybe I will fix me tomorrow, no he said I will fix myself NOW and he did. First order of business being more giving and treating those in his life as he should have always treated them with love and respect even paying them fairly. Being a miser and pay all too often people accept a modern day miser and feel well I deserve this and we do not, we accept misers and shouldn't.

Scrooge I believe once had a large heart especially when he worked for Fezziwig, he seemed so happy and cheerful even having love in his life but along the way went astray. Something that happens to all of us, going astray, darker, cold and heartless until we wake up but look what it took for Scrooge to wake up, what will it take for you and I to wake up to be kinder, softer and more loving.

Scrooge continues to be watched in my home every year and different versions, but my favorite by far is the 1954 version with Alastair Sims what a perfect Scrooge, but I am also partial to Reginald Owens and Michael Caine in Muppets Christmas Carol. I know this season we tend to stay indoors a lot even more so today watching our favorite classics, all seem to have message of the hardships of holidays, but ultimately coming to almost the same conclusion to be kinder, love more, look to what is important in life so why can't people just do it. People make the choice not to because frankly people love living in the dark, being mean, cold towards others feeling there is no reward to being kind, but there is a reward our soul is rewarded.

So make Christmas 2024 a time to remember what is important, LOVE, KINDNESS and Peace on Earth each of us have the ability to do these things if we just try making the world less hateful, bitter. Ultimately, I will say this the reason for season as always is to remember Jesus was born to die on this day and his birth is the reason for the season, a ultimate sacrifice to all of us, but the ultimate love for all of us, so lets try to love more like Christ. Regardless if you don't believe in CHRIST, we can all be much kinder to each other.

Peace to all in this time and Merry Christmas!

11 Today in the town of David a Savior has been born to you; he is the Messiah, the Lord.

Luke 2:11

Part IV – On Writing

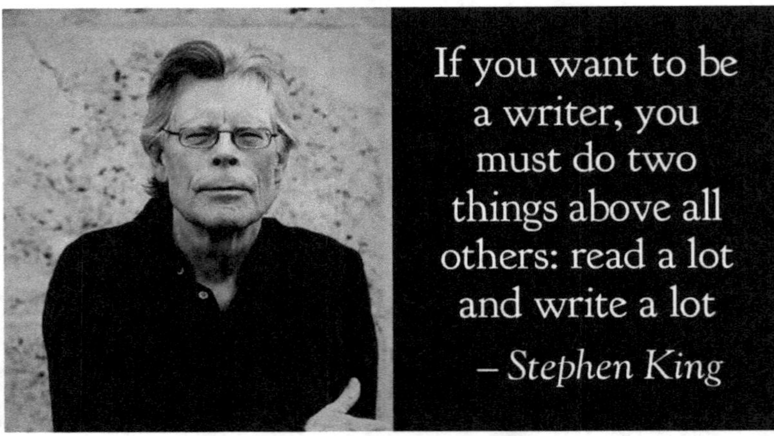

Chapter 35

In The Works, My Writing

February 10, 2024

My writing continues to take off as I expand my writing in many different ways such as in my blogging, my books and other media like my podcast and vlogs on YouTube.

My stories consume my mind each day as I am anxious to complete them but they take time. I am currently working on the following:

1. My 2nd Novel "The Menagerie", which will be coming out March 17th. This is my first attempt at a paranormal genre which centers around a circus. My different influences have gone into this work from my love of the circus to my fascination with the paranormal and the supernatural.

2. Currently writing the follow up to my debut novel “The Pox” to bring back my main character Dr. Jack Spellman. This book takes place right after the last book and will continue as this Dystopian book filled with mystery and thrillers. This book will mostly not be ready until 2025 or early 2026 as I am still writing it but anticipate it will be much larger than the Pox and may be a long novel, but I saw see if I surprise myself with packing a good punch of a book.
3. Currently writing my memoir about my life and the struggles I have experienced in my life up to this point. This book will have a faith element to it as it also focusses on my faith and how GOD has impacted my life. I am thinking I will have this book ready by January 2025.
4. Currently creating a book of my childhood short stories that I wrote when I was twelve years old. These stories were originally featured in my early blog posts from “Stories from Child’s past” series. This book I will also look to include some simple illustrations since many of stories involve characters. I am unsure when this book will be ready, but I could possibly be in 2025.
5. New short story in the works as I have begun to write a short story, but it could turn into a novel, this is another work in progress.

My writing is a big part of my life as each time I publish, it is a great accomplishment and another piece of work I give the world access too. Most importantly my writing is not just for myself but for a way I can leave my legacy to my wife, daughter, and family. Who knows I may be the next Tolkien or King, for future generations to read, a man can only hope. I will continue to keep writing as like all writers are voices are created within the pages we create. Until then I will keep writing!

Chapter 36

The Circus is Coming To Town in My Book

February 18, 2024

The circus is coming to town **March 17th, 2024** with my newest novel **The Menagerie Locket**. A book takes place in a circus, but a circus with secrets that will soon be discovered.

THE MENAGERIE LOCKET
This Is No Ordinary Circus
JOE R. MEYER

This book takes you into one of my favorite themes, subjects with characters I hope leap off the page. This book infuse mystery, Mysticism, paranormal and so much more without giving it all away.

More details to come when its official available on all the major sights and when you can begin to purchase as it will be both in e-book and paperback.

Welcome to the Circus

Chapter 37

Rest in Christ Pastor Jeff Johnson, 1948-2024

February 18, 2024

I find myself sorrowful today finding out that the pastor who brought me to the Lord had passed, which obliviously new what happen one day, he was 76 years old. Going home on **February 13th, 2024**.

Although I did not know this man person, attending Calvary Chapel was my home church for many years but it in 2008/2009 when I was invited by a friend/co worker at the time, the same friend who introduced me to my future wife.

Having attended church before brought up in a Baptist church my grandparents attended which still stands today. Then later in life as a teenage going full catholic at St. Pixus in Santa Fe Springs, California. Finally landing at Calvary Chapel Downey where I gave my heart to the lord, where I cried many times as I struggle with a new relationship, working towards being a better man and eventually husband and father.

What makes this church and the pastor so special was that my mother Linda Gutierrez attended with me and my wife and on her own before she passed in 2015, having her bible where she left notes. I fully trust she is with the

Lord now in paradise, and I look forward to seeing her one day.

Pastor Jeff who had a long history with Calvary chapel once a drug dealer, giving his life to the Lord, having tried every form of spirituality before coming to the lord. Like anyone else he was growing older when I first came to his church as he was already in his sixties but still full of incredible words, energy and love for GOD.

From my time there I went full Christian, going to Sunday, Wednesday services, Men's bible studies on Thursday nights. I will say this was definitely a different time in my life and he help get me through those times, as I often found comfort in the pews of his large church.

The church now in hands of Art Reyes, who I find to be a great choice not only by Pastor Jeff but the Lord as I regularly watch.

Pastor Jeff was married to his wife Karyn, having children but leaving behind so much more, his incredible impact on the hearts of men, women and children as he goes home in the arms of the lord as I imagine the lord saying

"Well done, my faithful servant". Matthew 25:23.

Pastor Jeff also wrote a book called "The Seeker" Which I have personally read that anyone would enjoy reading about such a great man: https://www.amazon.com/Seeker-Johnsons-Search-Clear-Light/dp/1931667683

Chapter 38

More To Come, My Writing Journey

February 21, 2024

I'm proud that I get to publish my work independently although I would love to be considered by the book world as a known author like Stephen King whose books reach millions and instantly turned into films and television.

As an independent author I love that I can get my work, my passion to the public almost instantly. I'll admit it would be a dream to have representation like an agent and publisher but maybe one day.

In the meantime I'm going to keep writing, bringing my passion to the world myself. For those who don't know , here are my two published works.

The Pox , pub. 06-18-23

The Menagerie Locket , pub. 03-17-24

Thank you for all those who support me, encourage me each day. If you have a passion for writing your own book, you can , don't be an afraid and you won't regret it, it may be lifesaving for you like it is for me.

Chapter 39

The Circus is in Town March 17th

Original title: The Circus is in Town March 17th: New Book, The Menagerie Locket

March 13, 2024

Do you love the circus, even the ones that are filled intrigue, mystery and maybe a little tragedy or a lot , Then **Fucini's Family Circus** may be just your ticket to the greatest show on earth west of the Mississippi.

Come see lions, tigers, clowns and the stars the Freak!

Stay after the show for something truly spine tingling special after dark, but beware you just might not be able to leave.

THE MENAGERIE LOCKET
This Is No Ordinary Circus
JOE R. MEYER

Chapter 40

Short Stories from a Child's Mind

April 26, 2024

As once a twelve old writer, I would often sit and write short stories, depending on the mood I was in, whether I wrote about animals, historical figures or monsters. I am now bringing those short stories to the world in book form as I provide short synposis of the stories I wrote along with the actual image of those stories.

SHORT STORIES FROM A CHILD'S MIND
Animal Friends Edition
By Joseph Gutierrez
SHORT STORIES FROM A CHILD'S MIND
Swashbuckler & Gunslinger Edition
Coming Soon
SHORT STORIES FROM A CHILD'S MIND
The Monster's Edition
BY JOSEPH GUTIERREZ

Each edition will be released in May, June and July, giving each a glimpse into my mind as a child, so come along and take a journey with me.

Chapter 41

Living in The WP World

Original title: Living in The WP World, The Refuge of My Breaking Mind

May 20, 2024

Do you ever feel like WordPress is the only place we can truly express ourselves without judgment and fear as we can literally talk about anything. I love how I can write about what I am struggling with and there will be some who comment, some who like my posts, but at the end of the day we live in this secret world that many probably choose to ignore only to focus on other medians like Tik Tok, X, Facebook and others. I am not coming here for followers, although its nice when others follow my posts.

I am more interested in my freedom to say what I like and not have the world judge me. For example, I could never put on LinkedIn that I struggle with mental health at times, or about how I attempted to end my life many years ago or how I feel worthless each day and still think about ending my life in the future. I could never say on LinkedIn that I feel that although I love my job and the people there, that in the end it really doesn't matter or how I just want to run away because I feel lost. (Can you name the reference to what I just said)

WP is my refuge , my therapy from my thoughts, but also my writing of books, short stories, blogs allows me to explore my mind to utmost degree. This is where I lay my history of who I am each day, putting my heart out here for the world or even WP world to see.

Thank you to all those who listen to my rants, that to others I probably sound like a man on the edge, a lunatic who is on the verge of losing it. I promise I will not lose it just yet, I have a lot to say in my books, blogs, Pods and VLOGS as I work to leave my history behind one day, so my family has something to listen, read and watch instead of existence disappearing in oblivion.

At this point I feel broken right now, I am doing the best I can but pray for my state of mind to be okay. I am not okay right now, but will try to push forward.

Chapter 42

What Would You Sacrifice for Your Heart's Desire?

September 30, 2024

My newest horror novel out October 2nd, Pounds of Flesh is a tale of great sacrifice to get something your heart desires which is different for everyone. So I ask what would you do for your Pounds of Flesh to get what your heart desires, What does your heart desire? Money, Wealth, Fame, Beauty and the list goes on. Or would you selflessly want something for someone you love or loved.

Follow Jacoby Henriksen on his torturous journey as he get his Pounds of Flesh for redemption and the life he once had making the deal of life time.

A HORROR NOVEL
POUNDS
OF
FLESH
GET YOUR POUNDS OF FLESH, BUT YOU MAY REGRET IT
JOE R. MEYER

Chapter 43

Scary Titles To Scare You into the Spooky Season!

Original title: Scary Titles To Scare You into the Spooky Season! Get your copy today

October 6, 2024

Looking for a good scare, check out decades of scares from short stories (Written when I was 12 years old) to my more recent publications.

Whether you are a fan of blood, monsters and ghouls or the Paranormal, each having the perfect scare for your taste.

Chapter 44

Self-Publishing My Autobiography

Original title: Self-Publishing My Autobiography: The Forgotten Boy

October 27, 2024

It gives me pleasure in announcing I have completed the first draft of my autobiography and memoire, which took me over a year to write the first draft coming out to close to 145K words, but that is just the beginning as I will surely be adding pictures and additional chapters like the forwards and afterwards.

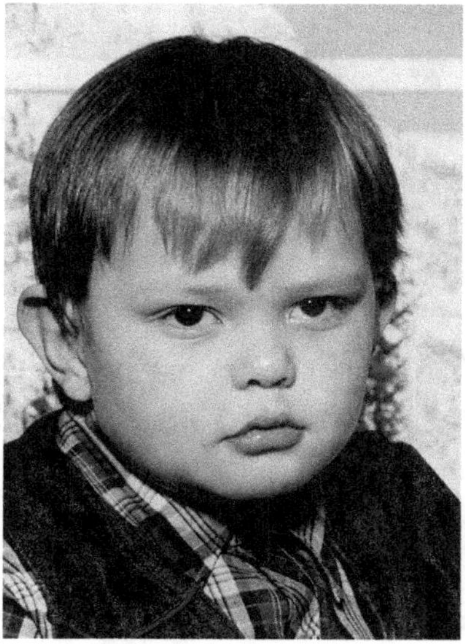

Deciding to break it down into two books actually such as the early years and later years up to date. This book was very personal to me as I put all out there and once I publish give those who read it , the picture of me, my thoughts, values and my life.

One may think that why would someone like myself write a autobiography, I am a nobody, not a celebrity or public figure, what could I possibly bring to the world in my words. The truth is I didn't write for myself, but really meant to be a historical account of my life for my wife and daughter, so if it in the case I am no longer here, they will have a history, an ancestry to look back at.

I am most likely going to title the book "The Forgotten Boy" with some addition of Chapter 1 and 2 or the first book will just be the "The Forgotten Boy" and the second will have chapter 2. This may sound familiar as what is done in movies and films that have multiple parts, like one of my favorite films "IT", breaking it out in two books. I contemplated making it one book, but really each book has its own focus.

I am going to let the book breath for a little bit before I begin the editing process and see where I go from there. Hopefully I can get the first book self-published by early to mid next year and the 2nd part in later half of the year.

Chapter 45

The Pox Lives On: Exciting Updates and a New Cover

November 11, 2024

The Pox my debut novel has is apart of me and will forever be apart of me. Although I would like to think my debut novel was finished, I have went back and found ways to improve. Being that this was my first attempt at self publishing felt it was best to honor my book with a second edition, a revised version and a better cover.

The Pox lives on as I am currently editing the follow up to the Pox which will be out in 2025 and I look forward to introducing that novel to the world.

Here is the front and back cover I intend to introduce in January 2025.

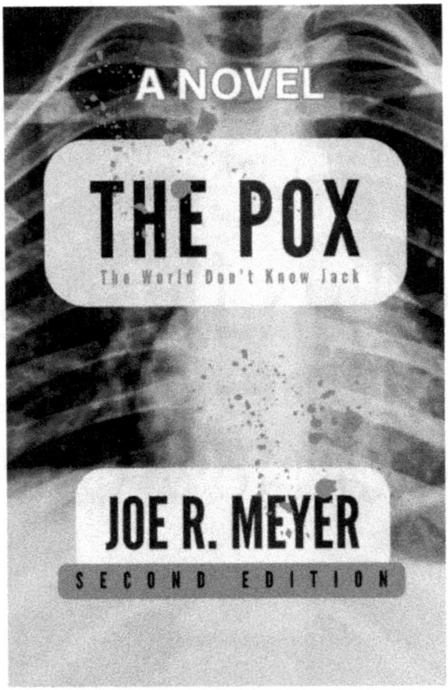

For those who wanted to see the difference from Old Cover to new, see below:

Chapter 46

The Stricken: A New Chapter in The Pox Series

Original title: The Stricken: A New Chapter in The Pox Series Launching Jan 20, 2025

November 17, 2024

It gives me great pleasure to announce the saga of Doctor Jack Spellman continues of the The Pox.

The follow up to The Pox, which was written in 2019, published in 2023.

The next chapter called The Stricken will be out January 20th, 2025, Inauguration day!

This book is a long read, similar in nature to the first original drafts of the Pox. The book will be available at all major online retailers like Amazon and Barnes and Noble.

A NOVEL
THE
STRICKEN
JACK IS BACK & HE'S OUT FOR BLOOD
JOE R. MEYER

Chapter 47

The Stricken: A Riveting Sequel

Original title: The Stricken: A Riveting Sequel in an Intriguing Saga

November 25, 2024

The Pox and The Stricken have been apart of my writing journey since 2019. Creating a world that we all pray we never are apart of as this saga includes mystery, adventure, crime and a world that exists behind the scenes.

The Stricken I hope is a worthy follow up as a writer my work is never finished which is why I came out with a second edition of the Pox both out for pre-sale on December 9th.

A NOVEL
THE POX
JOE R. MEYER
A NOVEL
THE STRICKEN
JOE R. MEYER
Joe R. Meyer Creatives Presents
THE POX HAS JUST BEGUN
Doctor Jack Spellman and the saga of the Pox and the Stricken rage on, are you ready?
Pre-sale Dec 9th
MD

Chapter 48

Pre-Order Today and Get Stricken with the Pox

Original title: Pre-Order Today and Get Stricken with the Pox, you may regret it!

December 12, 2024

The Pox (Second Edition) and the Follow up The Stricken, is now on pre-sale and ready to hit virtual shelves January 20th, that's right Inauguration day which is fitting for the Stricken.

Writing this Dystopian tale was difficult, as I put my imagine to the test of a world that I hope never exists, but sadly we are going into our own Dystopian world in the future years. Something that should only be written about and not lived, as is the case with Orwell's 1984 and Animal Farm, both incredible classics.

Pre-order your copy today from start to finish with the Pox and The Stricken. Available through all major online retailers.

Part V – Family

Chapter 49

Happy Birthday, Love

March 18, 2024

Happy Birthday to my love, my wife , my partner, my Best Friend Delia who I am eternally grateful for your love and sacrifice each day taking care of me and our daughter.

I know it cant be easy with me at times, with all my moods, my happy state, my depressive state, but I love you and thank GOD each day you are in my life and I get to share another birthday with you.

As your husband, I am sorry I can not take you on fancy vacations, bye you expensive gifts and although you say you don't need those things, I still wish so much to give them to you and sorry to say since I can't I do feel as husband I have failed you.

Thank you for loving me unconditionally each day, Being my support and my rock and like I have told you many times, you saved me so many years ago coming into my life and without you, I do not know where I would be. I fight my internal demons each day to be a better husband, father and friend, but thank you for loving me. I feel prilvaged to spend our days together, to grow older with you as I see your beautiful heart grow larger and larger for me and our daughter, I love you to the ends of the earth and back.

Happy Birthday!

Chapter 50

Constant Reflections on Life

March 22, 2024

I often reflect on the state of my mind as at times I feel like I am going into madness, unpredictability and on edge, which I feel most of the time. I feel defensive now this point in my life, like when is something going to be taken from me, like money, my job, my health.

My Daughters Generation is Nothing like mine

I can not help looking around and attempting to compare today's times to those of the age my daughter Mikaylah is which is age 11. It would have been 1991 when I was age 11, living In Bell Gardens, California or as renamed it Bell Garbage.

Reflections of Yesteryear

I was in the 5th grade most likely, going to Suva Intermediate, home of the Bull dogs. I was the fat kid like I am today, instead I see myself as the fat man.

Being the Fat Kid Was Painful

I was a sweet kid, shy, reserved, tried to keep to myself, in my own world not having many friends from what I remember, sticking to myself on most days. I would like to write, doddle and wander, as I loved to wander around the school on breaks and lunch as I attempted to explore different parts of the school.

I lived with my mother, sister and grandfather, who I call Devil, since that is what he resembled with this verbal torture he would inflict on me , my sister and mother every single day with no peace in the house, as we constantly be told we need to keep the house keep, pick up after the dogs, make sure we kids were quiet and never, ever were we talk back or else, punishment.

Mom, Our Defender

Mom constantly defended my sister and I having blow outs at times with the Devil, but we never left as mom needed us kids to have a roof and it was hard for her, god bless her tried, working hard, but it didn't seem to be a enough.

I made it point never to treat my own family like that, but there are things I have my moods, my moods come more frequently as I come home, tired, having to get ready for my 2nd job at 6pm Monday – Thursday, with little time just to sit down and relax and enjoy time to myself.

I feel I have really let my family down at times as I don't spend enough quality time with them as I work full time and part time, leaving me little for anything else and Mom/wife works in the evenings most of the week.

The Changing Seasons of Life

I had an opportunity last year to have more freedom with a full time that paid me much more, where I could have technically had one job and we would have been okay, but I blew those opportunities, because I am an idiot who couldn't decide, taking one of the jobs that end up being a mistake , having to leave, start the job search all over again, finally leading me to where I am today. The money is still good, but not as great as the other two jobs.

Being Thankful

I am thankful for work, because frankly one never knows when the gravy train will stop. Thankful I am still fairy young at 44 and able bodied, still with enough fuel in my tank to go many more years, but that is not up to me, but GOD to keep me healthy, employed, and okay.

The Fear of Aging

I fear when I get old and if I am out of work past fifty as by then I would be considered past my prime in this world as we for the most part reject people over fifty and forget about 60 and above, you are basically useless to companies despite having all your facilities, to society your garbage, a young man or woman's game at that point.

If that was to happen to me at that age and society rejects me in the workforce, I would definitely call it a day and that would be end, a sure sign from GOD that my time has come. Although many would argue not to give up, keep pushing forward, go for the gold, you'll get another job, but Nah Society, especially ours is ruthless discarding people due to age and viability.

For now, I will hold tight as I feel I have usefulness, but only time will tell as I see so many fighting to survive to live, but I ask why. Who can endure being unemployed for 8,9, 12, months or more that is unacceptable in a society who is supposed be well advanced with plenty of work to go around, but no employers have other plans in who they want in their offices, very selective choices that have nothing to do with skills, but physical appearance.

Sizeism Exist and hurts many

Studies have shown in live in a world of ageism, sizeism (https://www.nature.com/articles/d41586-022-01536-y#:~:text=Despite%20this%2C%20weight%20discrimination%20is,over%20the%20past%20few%20decades.) , racism, where it is my belief that those Caucasian , taller and more European looking have no problem finding work despite their age as society tends to see them as more valuable, something I've personally witnessed but the argument is well they must be qualified but even in society you look those higher profile individuals in business and politics who do great harm but are allows too such as people like Musk and Bezos, Gates, and others who are allowed to get alway with doing and saying as they wish despite the harm that's caused, another current example is Trump.

Times, They are a Changing

Today I see the change in times each day and although we all human, different generations shape the lives and workplace of others because they are the majority now. I see Gen Z, Alpha and boy they seem uninhibited, free to act and say what they want and feel my generation X was often not allowed, told to follow the rules, which have seemed to disappear. I guess it's good that the generations of today feel they can express themselves in different ways in society and the workplace.

Don't know what the Future holds

I don't know what my future looks like but I will attempt to appreciate my age, my experience and where I am today, but can't help to feel little value to society as younger generations have surpassed me in so many ways like wealth, but there are areas we have gone back in time too like having conversations with people, reading, writing, the basics at times as many are addicted to their devices, wrapped up in the lives of celebrities, influencers who appear to have better lives then you, but looks can be deceiving as how many of people have we seen kill themselves confusing me in how can someone who appears to have everything do that like money, fame, good health and the lists goes on.

A failure in my eyes

I ask myself each day how did I get to this point in life , how did I survive? Imagining if I had succeeded so many years ago where my soul would be right now, thankful, but unable to help feeling disappointed in my self , which is constant and it's not that i don't feel appreciative or grateful for the things I do have but fail in this life on different levels especially financially , and I see myself as a poor provider despite my family having a roof over our head, food, clothing and the necessities but every little excess.

Self Aware on so many levels

I will continue to self reflect, in hopes of being the best me, but the negativity and self deprivation will never end as my mind will not be at rest until some miracle happens or I'm no longer earth bound but heaven bound.

Until my next rant, stay tuned because my mind can be triggered any moment now.

Chapter 51

Happy Mother's Day!

May 11, 2024

Happy Mother's Day! To all the moms of all types of especially grandmothers, Dad's we get our next month, but let's celebrate mom's as we should celebrate them each and every day for the sacrifices they make. I get that mom's will just be mom's and to do what they got to do to feed the family, to put food on the table and often women who are mother's do not get all the appreciation and respect they deserve.

I have many mothers in my life, in my personal life and home life. But two that hold the title to the best mom's, my wife Delia, and my mother Linda (Who passed in 2015). My mother who, if not for her I would not be in this world today, who through her life made sacrifices, often going without herself, putting myself sister and I first, which is what parents do. I didn't realize until I got old how much she gave up, especially her chance at a career and I feel some of her life's goals were squashed. I can no longer repay my mother for all that she did, but when she was here, I knew she loved me, my wife and of course her granddaughter Mikaylah, getting to see and spend time with her before she passed.

Growing up we always tended to celebrate this special day with traditional flowers, a meal and gifts and I gladly pass on that tradition to my daughter and wife who we celebrate each year, because these memories are precious.

My wife and the mother of our daughter Mikaylah is the person who I get to show how important she is and one day a year is not enough as she makes too many sacrifices for us especially working a physically taxing job each week, something that pains me because she should be a job that she can not relax at times. I'll admit I don't always show her the appreciation she deserves as life brings me down along with my own struggles, but I love her, appreciate you and am thankful for her love for myself and our daughter.

It pains me each day I cannot give her the life she deserves as she deserves a mansion, a million, no a billion bucks in the bank just for her, a life of leisure and peace. I often show her my love but could do better as parents we know our daughter is a gift and want the best for her.

This day may not be a celebration for everyone, as there are some truly horrible mothers out there who abused their gifts, and yes children are a gift from God and mother's neglect, abuse, murder, kill, abuse and have the ability to cause so much pain to their kids where, their impact can be so much more harmful than a father, especially an absent father.

If you mom is your life, love her , appreciate her, cherish her because you never know when she just wont be there anymore.

Chapter 52

Health Issue Here, Keep Me In Prayer

June 10, 2024

The plight of my struggles is ongoing at times if I am not dealing with my mental health on a daily basis or financial, I am dealing with a health issue unexpectedly.

Over the last couple of weeks, I have experienced strange things with my vision suddenly, as in the right eye I was seeing floaties and swirls, trippy things, thinking at first it must be equated to me getting older, although I am only 44 years old. Although my vision has never been great, I could see fine with glasses.

It was this week, when I felt my vision change, where I was still able to see, but did an eye test myself, covering my right and left eye.

Covering my right eye, I could see normal even when not wearing my glasses, but when I covered my left eye, it was all fuzzy, where I couldn't read or see anything, it was a blur, appearing as if my eye was under water.

I immediately scheduled an appointment with my eye doctor, and it was determined that my Retina had detached, and I would need to now see an ophthalmologist to have this right repaired.

This is certainly frightening, having never experienced this issue with my eye before. Based on what I have researched, it's fixable with no pain, but minor discomfort, but still inconvenient, but beats losing sight in one eye. I believe I caught it early enough to get corrected but think If I waited or decided not to correct, it would have gotten worse and irreversible.

Keep me in your prayers and for those interested in what the heck I am speaking of here is article.

Retinal detachment - Symptoms and causes - Mayo Clinic

Retinal detachment describes an emergency situation in which a thin layer of tissue (the retina) at the back of the eye pulls away from its normal position.

Retinal detachment separates the retinal cells from the layer of blood vessels that provides oxygen and nourishment to the eye. The longer retinal detachment goes untreated, the greater your risk of permanent vision loss in the affected eye.

Chapter 53

Happy Father's Day 24'

June 15, 2024

As a father of my 11-year-old daughter, I have been given the gift of parenthood and yes it's a gift although some may not think it is. It's the most meaningful job I have to today, next to be a husband. Changing my life forever in January 2013.

I often reflect on my own father Moses, as my parents were divorced, I would spend every other weekend with my sister with him at my grandparents' house, where he lived as well. My father, who often worked graveyard shifts, would be too exhausted to spend time with my sister and I at times.

Although my father is still alive today and still in my life, he was distant in offering fatherly advice, often substituting time for money, purchasing toys and food such as taking us to Chuck E Cheese and letting us often roam free doing what we wanted when we were at our grandparents house which included eating and drinking whatever we wanted such as drinking as much soda as we like, eating junk food galore and watching as much tube as we wanted. My grandparents stepped in a lot and attempted to inform us about what to eat and how much television time we could get. He would also take us to all the latest films, especially horror films that were not age appropriate.

Yes, by the sound of it, we were not really parented, and I know the way I describe my father seems like I am putting him down, but that is who he was and is today. Do I believe he loves my sister and I, well I sure hope so.

When it comes to my own daughter, she is of a different generation and is apart of the IPAD generation or Alpha generation where she lives off her iPad speaking with friends, playing games and chatting.

From the time she was born, I have been there every moment to watch those huge milestones like first words, first steps and first everything. Being a father has changed my life in so many ways, it has allowed me to have a different perspective about myself and put her first along with my life.

In the time of being a father it also was one of the most challenging and stressful times as I worked to keep food on the table and a roof over our head. I will say that having a family and a daughter has allowed me to self on my own failures as a father.

I know there are far worse off fathers out there, I personally have lived in a house of hell with a grandfather who put down, demoralized his own daughter, my mother, who I would never consider a grandfather, the devil himself in my eyes.

One of the reasons I think fathers get so little appreciation at times is because many, far too many fathers have failed their children, who have abandoned them, hurt them, physically, emotionally, verbally and done damage that cannot be undone.

For those who know me or don't know me, reading my blogs may see me as someone who is conscious about what I am as a provider, a person, a father and husband and in every instance, I see I have failed them, they deserve so much better.

I pray one day I can truly mimic the real father Jesus and his goodness, his beauty, but I will never be like Jesus, there is only one Jesus. What I will do for now is admire the good dads out there, who are true provider, who rock it at their careers and lives , who are incredible husbands, offering their family all their heart desires , being a man their family can not live without, I don't think I am that man.

I know this is a strange Father's day message, But Happy Father's Day!

Chapter 54

Wallows Concert Experience at Kia Forum

Original title: Wallows Concert Experience at Kia Forum: A Generation's Impact

September 14, 2024

This week, I had the pleasure and honor of taking my daughter Mikaylah who is 11 years old to her first concert, an Alternative rock band called the Wallows (Wallows - Wikipedia). A Group that orientated in Los Angeles started in 2017, signed to record deal in 2018. I had never heard of this group before, which is not uncommon being that I am creature of habit listing to my old favorites, metal, rock, 80's and 90's and 2000's. The music is light and has good rhythms and catchy tunes.

The concert takes place on September 12th at the Kia Forum, which was formally the Great Western Forum. A place I am familiar with once saw The Red-Hot Chili Peppers at the By The Way tour on October 11, 2003.

The Wallows consisting of band members Dylan Minnette, Braeden Lemasters and Cole Preston. The opening act was performed by a singer called Benee, which I thought was entertaining.

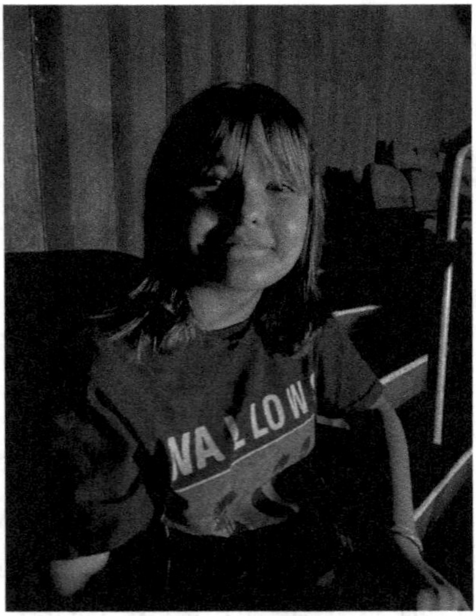

This experience was unlike anything I had experienced, although having been to concerts in my youth like Bon Jovi at the Have a Nice day Tour, Shania Twain, George Michael and other concerts that included different artist mostly apart of the KIIS FM radio station like Jingle Balls and Wango Tango, which we would go with my mother for the most part. Oh and I cant forget Gwen Stefani at her Harajuku Lovers Tour at the Hollywood bowl.

I have always loved music and the musical experience growing up and glad to see my glad appreciation of music. The Wallows tickets were purchased by my sister Jennifer as a Christmas/Birthday gift last year.

The Kia Forum, having not been there a very long time, appeared for the most part the same, but what was different was the experience. The parking lot filled with mostly young women, and men too in the age range of 14-30 for the most part. Standing around these young people, I couldn't help to observe the new generation of adults, many of which are generation Z's and Alphas, coming from my generation X.

Generation X raised a new breed of children much different then myself, almost shocking to me at first as I look around mostly women, who I found to be severely out of shape, obese and seemed to have great fluidity. The young women, dressed scantily, but many just dressed sloppy. I know my observation seems judgmental and harsh and many might say who am I to judge, am I perfect and no I am not perfect, I am overweight myself, but these are much younger people who have developed poor habits.

I remember when I was around the age of this young adults 24-28, remembering my own youth as this was a time of great struggle for me as I searched often for friendships and love, rejected mostly for the most part. I reason I bring this up is because I looked around at this concert and found that many of the young men who were much larger than men, appearing to have found love themselves, accepted for who they are, despite their human physical flaws.

Reminded How FAT I AM

I was ALWAYS reminded how FAT I was, how disgusting I was because I was overweight and fat and rejected by women. These women they were not special, average women with average intelligence. While myself I was educated, with a bachelors and master's and somewhat successful at this age, but was undesirable.

What was painful too was that younger people seemed to be more accepting of their bodies, due to toxic body positivity movements that have taken place over the years. Back at this age, I couldn't find a girlfriend yet alone to have a girl just look at me, desire me, appreciate me for who I was, this was and is very painful to think about. Even though I am married today with a wife who loves me, that rejection hit me deep and scared me for life.

Due to this rejection I grew to hate myself, my body, feeling grotesque, which is one of the reasons I felt I spiraled out of control mentally, leading to one of the reasons I attempted to take my life.

Sitting in row 15, upper level sitting at the top with no one sitting behind us, which was nice, the view was not bad. Sitting with my Mikaylah, Jennifer, myself and Delia (Wife/Mother). Being the people watcher myself, a very large women sat next to me, large thighed women with a man, mostly likely her boyfriend, but I saw no signs of affection, they mostly just sat and watched.

But looking around, there where a group of women who sat in front of us, large, obese women who were friends, having a good time. They were not the only ones as there we many younger people who struggled to walk to and down the steep steps carrying more weight than I would prefer or recommend. One would say why do I care, let people live their own lives, let people be who they want to be.

Body Positivity has ruined a generation

I get the argument, if people are happy as are, fat and all, what do I care, its not my body, not my life and all valid arguments. I think about how we as society became so less concerned about obesity and unhealthy lifestyles, when unhealthiness was cramped down my generations throat which most likely led to many people hating fat people, overweight people, causing harm, mental harm to people like me who never saw themselves good enough to be loved.

There was also something important I realized at this point too, seeing people living their lives and that I had wasted my youth. At that age especially when I was 27 years old, when I attempted to end my life. My life has gotten better and worse over the years, I did find love, having my daughter who I love, but when I look at my daughter, I never want her to feel the way I do, rejected. Humans and people are quite cruel to each other. Why was it so hard for someone to just spend time with me, I don't know but I tried greatly.

I am thankful I did get to experience this with my daughter, she had a great time , a great memory that she will never forget. Although my experience was not the best because frankly I could not even stand due to the large women, going into my lane, preferring to sit down and making attempts to watch the big screen, but in reality I was not there for me, it was for Mikaylah and her joy, mission accomplished.

This concert surely changed my perception, by beliefs in a way as I reflected on my own life, who would have thought a concert could do that as I see what a waste of life I had in my youth and how I had failed at those ages with no friends, lonely, searching for love and rejected, a painful remainder of this concert.

I also realized that many of those in the sea of crowds looked happy, something I wish I could have experienced at their age and even today, as I fall slowly in despair each day, knowing that I can never go back to those days.

Looking back to past can be painful, full of regrets, this concert will be a reminder of that.

Chapter 55

Rosalie Eleanor Nerio (1944 - 2024)

Original title: Rosalie Eleanor Nerio (1944 - 2024): A Life of Love, Caring, and Enduring Legacy

September 16, 2024

Rosalie Eleanor Nerio was an incredibly kind women, who I grew up with and as a child, always had a youthfulness about her. She loved to laugh and talk, she was a real chatter box who loved to talk to our late mother Linda, in which they would talk for hours and hours.

Rosalie Eleanor Nerio, born on September 21, 1944, Los Angeles, California, passed away on May 3, 2024, in Whittier, California. Rosie is remembered for her loving and caring nature, as well as her of character. She was surrounded by family and close friends who prayed for her peaceful transition to Heaven.

She worked alongside her husband at their family business, Mission Market, before pursuing a career at Sears in Los Angeles. Once she had children, Rosie dedicated herself to being a stay-at-home mom, actively volunteering at her children's school as a Room Mom and Den Leader. Later in life, she returned to school, earning her certificate in Child Health and Education from Rio Hondo College, allowing her to work in local child day care centers.

Rosie's hobbies reflected her joy in life; she loved swimming, playing outside with friends as a child, and enjoyed baking, cooking, and crafting with her children as a mother and grandmother. Family gatherings, road trips, and excursions to the casino brought her much happiness. Even as a senior, she cherished conversations on the phone and writing and receiving letters from loved ones.

Rosie's remarkable memory made her an excellent storyteller, and she had a rare ability to strike up a conversation with anyone, quickly turning strangers into friends. Her kindness meant that she was always willing to help others, even if just in small ways.

Rosalie Nerio is survived by her siblings: Donald Meyer and his wife Carolyn, Dorothy Allen, and Carolyn Loya. She leaves behind her children: Genevive Nerio Castillo and her husband Dominic, Arthur Nerio and his wife Suzanne, and John A. Nerio.

Her legacy continues through her grandchildren: Jillian Barger and Scott Barger, Lauren Renee Smith and James Smith, Jamie Alexandria Castillo Ramahi and Safadyn Ramahi, Nicholas Anthony Castillo Castro and Marisa Castro, and Luke M. Castillo.

Her great-grandchildren include Brigham Michael Barger, Ellie Renee Barger, and Anita Rose Smith.

She was preceded in death by her parents, Florian and Anne Meyer, her husband Nicholas C. Nerio, her siblings Joan Garcia and Joseph Meyer, and her daughter-in-law Connie Nerio.

A memorial service will be held on September 18, 2024, from 5 PM to 8 PM at the White Emerson Mortuary located at 13304 Philadelphia St, Whittier, CA 90601.

Funeral Mass will be held the next morning, September 19, 2024 at 10:00 am at Our Lady of Perpetual help at 8545 Norwalk Blvd, Whittier, CA 90606

https://www.whiteemerson.com/obituaries/rosalie-nerio

Chapter 56

Celebrating 14 Years Together

Original title: Gratitude and Growth: Celebrating 14 Years Together

October 2, 2024

It has been 14 great years filled with love, laughter, and support. I am very thankful for my wife these years supporting me as we struggle at times, most financially but still encouraging me to keep reaching for the stars.

Over the years like any person I know I have changed a lot since first meeting in 2008 and I apologize that those changes are not always good changes, as my mental health over the years has taken a real toll on me and our marriage as I struggle with feeling as though I am a good husband and father, but deep down in my heart I feel I have failed her in many ways.

In my heart, she deserves so much better than me, but I am thankful to GOD for placing her in my life and I love her and she loves me.

I give credit to her, because I would probably not be here today if not for her as she gave me second life to rebuild and to find love.

May God bless our marriage for many years, giving me the strength to be a better husband and father to them both!

Chapter 57

A Personal Reflection on Motherhood

Original title: Honoring Sacrifice: A Personal Reflection on Motherhood

May 11, 2025

A special day for many, but for many it is not a day they choose to remember or take part in for many different personal reasons, maybe your mother is no longer here, maybe she was never in your life to begin with, maybe she chooses to leave your life or was a terrible mother in many senses of words.

For myself, my mother who I love and loved as she passed away in December 2015, making an impact in my life like no other, she self-sacrifice, her love and her struggles. Mom always seemed to struggle in life and not with drugs and/or alcohol but financially, being on the strict budget, not making very much at times, but always there as she would often work at our elementary school and high school as a teacher's aid. Unfortunately, due to what I would think was a low salary depended on her father, my grandfather who I have nicknamed the devil, as we were under his rulership for most of my childhood and teenage years and even into adulthood, mom lived under his rulership until she died. Although we didn't have money, she always provided food, clothes, time and love for my sister and I, which is all that mattered.

Today Mother's Day has a different meaning as I am married with a daughter of my own Mikaylah to my Wife and Mother Delia whom I love and cherish. She is an incredibly mother, loving stern at times, but giving, sacrificial working a thankless part time job at McDonald, who is often unappreciated, spoken down to , mistreated by her co-workers and managers, but she does it for the love of me and our daughter, something I don't think I could do in the sense of working in a place so horribly mistreated. Yes, she will leave eventually, but she is a trooper, a soldier in the battle of fast food, forgotten, but not by me and our daughter because we know her sacrifice. My wife deserves the best in this world, gold, riches and flowers on this day but unfortunately I am only able to get her cards and flowers, which may seem like its enough and it's the thought that counts, which is true, but again she deserves so much more for what she does for our daughter each day and I love her for that.

I think I have to remember that at times I could be really judgmental to my own mother but putting my sister and I in a hell house, but I know she did her best to protect us, keep us sheltered and fed but it came at a huge cost. For many out there, maybe you HATE your mother, which Is hard for me to fathom, remembering that a mother is a person, a human being, deserving compassion, but again its hard to imagine as I know there are many horrible mothers out and have seen and met many of them, but in the remembering you, the child are a gift, despite your mothers failures. This Mother's Day, try not to hold on to that hate, anger, disappointment because again your mother is human and we all fail, some royally fail at the most important job given to them, that goes for fathers too, but that I will save for Father's Day.

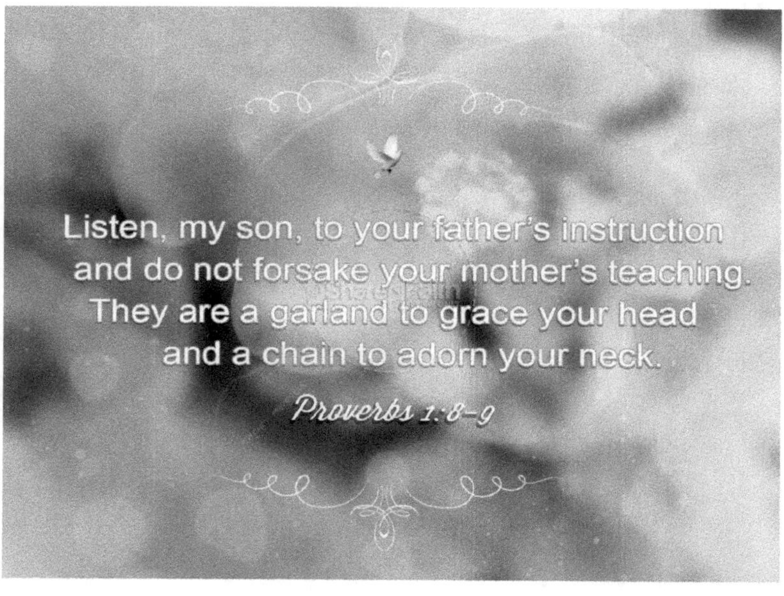

If your mother is in your life, love her, cherish her, tell her every single damn day, because frankly you never know when she may not be there. This day always brings me pain, knowing my mother was only 56 when she passed, taken from me too soon, anger at times that I see others who get to keep their mothers until old age, sharing holidays, birthdays and celebrations watching their grand kids grow up, something my daughter will never know. But I can save my festering for another day.

Chapter 58

Reflections on Fatherhood: A Complex Journey

June 14, 2025

As a father celebrates Father's Day, it can be complicated but not in the way one would think. You see of course, I grew up with my own father who is still living today named Moses. My own mother and father divorced when I was about five years old and my sister about three years old. Being that young as we grew up, we grew up living in two households. For the most part, we would see our father every other weekend and spend that time with him and our grandparents in Los Angeles.

My Own Father

My father whom I love, was not there in a way a father should be, yes he provide money for child support, yes, he purchase my clothes, toys, food and as we got older contributed to our adolescence in getting us what we needed, but mom was there very minute of the day for the most part.

My father growing up never really spoke to me about life, growing up and how to be a man, the meaning of life, all the big discussions a father should have with their son and children. I know I am not alone because there are many do didn't have a father growing up, possibly due to him leaving, abandonment and even death among the many, many reasons fathers are not in the picture and also simply because he didn't and doesn't want to be a father and maybe the mother doesn't want him in the picture, a million reasons.

Yes, I am fortunate to have my father in my life and grateful he was round. Unfortunately I had a another man in my life, who was no father figure, but one would you could call a grandfather who I lived with for most of my childhood and into adulthood, but he was a real devil of a man who to this day I remember the hate he spewed at myself, sister and mother every single damn day, may he rest in Hell.

Growing up, deep down I felt I wanted a father to take me and play ball, spend time with me, teach me things, but again, the man who attempted to be a father figure, force fed me his hate, vulgarity, anger and projection of his hate for my mom, sister and I each day and we stayed.

Although my mother is no longer living, she had her reasons, and I don't fault her for that, but the damage was done and she knew it.

Fatherhood

Today as a father of a daughter Mikaylah, I have attempted to rewrite the fathers in our life, but being there, supporting her and loving her each day and forever along with her mother, my wife Delia, whom I love. The problems lies that I am not a good father, I don't see myself as a good dad, in actuality I see myself as a failure of father, who failed to provide my daughter the life I promised her and she meant to have along with my life, as I consider myself a failure of a husband, a double whammy.

As far as I can remember, once I became a father, the greatest gift and joy a man could want. I know she is a gift from GOD, but I often think sadly did God Give this beautiful gift to the wrong person. I know its silly god doesn't make mistakes he is perfect.

Like stated in:

Psalm 127: 3-5 "**Behold, children are a heritage from the Lord, the fruit of the womb a reward**."

I can't help to think, my daughter deserves a much better father then me, she lucked out with me, as I look around at other dads. Dads who have better jobs, better job titles, make more money, offer better homes, provide all the needs and luxuries a father wants to give his children and partner, which allows a man to feel proud as a provider, but I am not.

Yes my daughter and wife had a roof over our heads, food on the table, but fancy vacations to Disney World, no vacations to fun and interesting place, but home bodies for the most part, a boring existence at times for myself, because I love to go out, spend quality time with my family, which one could say well, you don't need to go to a fancy vacation to do that, you can do that anywhere, who cares about expensive, bust your budget vacations, it's the love you share in the home that matters.

You see I have had these discussions with myself many many times before, and I come to same confusion, I failed my daughter, because every damn day it feels like a struggle with make sure everyone is okay, while my mental health, my well being suffers, pushing me closer and closer to the edge, making me realize my daughter and wife are simply just better off. As in my mind my wife could always remarry a better provider, which she vowed she would never do as she doesn't want other men in my daughter's life, but I give her my blessing.

You see although I don't have many friends, I have a few and, in my view, they are far better providers than myself. I often think of a friend of the families of my daughter, father and his wife, daughter and son, living in a beautiful home, working at Amazon and is able to provide without question for his family, even generously providing for my daughter at times, taking her and her friends to Disneyland, the mall, movies, out to eat, sparing no expense and I am eternally grateful. The other men in my life are co-workers, who are of different ages, basically we do the same type of work but at different stages in life and work, but in my view far superior providers.

I will take it a step further where men I don't even know as I go to the mall, shopping, out to eat as a master observer see what a great provider they are, just by looking at them. I know many of you may think I am being preposterous how in the hell would I know, how I can they are good providers just by looking at them, but in some sense I can. Even finding random men I find online, which again I know I sounds nuts, but I will stick with the men/fathers in my life I have direct contact with as I see them all better than me.

I see my only redemption in my future death with the possibility of a big life insurance policy that would pay upon death. As you can this is an antithesis of a Father's Day message and that is why I say Father's Day is completed. I wish I could just enjoy this day with a Father's Day lunch, gifts of appreciation and love, but even on the day alone, I am happy when the loved is shared with me by my wife and daughter, but at the same time when we go out, I cannot help other happy dads, enjoying their days. I often make some snide comment to my wife and daughter on this day about the "Happy Families" which usually angers them.

I Love being a dad, love my family, but at the end of the day believe they deserve better, and although I believe there are many shitty fathers today, I am not one of them, my deep rooted belief is I believe to be one.

Happy Father's day to all the incredible fathers out there, who know and believe your awesomeness, maybe one day I believe myself. God bless your day.

Chapter 59

Celebrating the Life and Legacy of My Late Mother

August 30, 2025

Happy Birthday Mom (Linda Gutierrez), it has been always ten years since you have been with us, but you are missing every day. You would have been celebrating your 66th birthday today. Imagining we would be celebrating your birthday simply at your favorite restaurant, Olive Garden, you were simple like that no fancy restaurants and I know there are better restaurants, but you loved it there. You would have myself, Mikaylah, your granddaughter, Delia, Jennifer (Sister) and Dad all together.

I know you would be so happy, but who knows what type of shape you would in as your health was not always good even when I was a young boy. But you always had a smile on your face, regardless of the hardship you struggled with, something I have learned from for myself over the years and trust me I have had a lot of hardships in this life.

You were always a giver, as a mom you would give me your last dime and did when you were alive. Mikaylah was the joy of your life as your first and only granddaughter, proud of Jennifer and I in what we had accomplished. What is amazing after all these years, you never know when your last day will be on earth, we honestly thought you would have lived for many more years, but that was not in God's plan for you as he had called you the heaven.

I know you are in heaven, because you gave your heart to Jesus, which gave me great comfort.

Although I would have loved for you to be here today, I understand it's not possible. I have attempted to not feel angry or jealous at times for you not here, when I see so many other families with grandparents, mothers and fathers who get to live long lives. Mikaylah also loves Olive Garden herself, like a chip off the old block, a remembrance and honor of you each time we go. Observing happy families with their grandmothers celebrating but I can't have that. I will not forget she has a grandmother today, Mama Conchi who we honor but lives in El Salvador, but she had gotten moments to spend and love Mikaylah, we are thankful for, a truly strong women to this day.

I look forward to the day I see you again in Heaven, until then I will honor and keep your memory alive so that your spirit lives on, but truthfully, I see so much of you in Mikaylah each day as if your spirit resides in her as if I am speaking to you. Not sure who believes but when our loved ones pass and go to Heaven, they watch over us like angels, but Jesus is our protector.

Love you,

Joseph

Chapter 60

Remembering Loved Ones: A Tribute to My Mother

December 9, 2025

Remembering My Mother, Linda

There are certain people in our lives that make an impact that once gone, you truly never feel the same, for me that person was my mother Linda who passed December 9th, 2015, making this the tenth year without mom.

Growing Up with Mom

Growing up with mom, she was always there, but at the same time, she always seemed to struggle with her health and financially, although if you looked at me as a child I was healthy, portly or fat as mom found a way to care for my sister and I, despite the fact we lived in the house of hell for most my upcoming, which is a common theme you will hear about in the trauma and damage inflicted on me growing up as I was most raised by my mother and grandfather who I refer to as the devil.

We always had a roof over our head and dad was in the picture and still today. I know mom loved me and my sister and would do anything for us like a mother's love.

Reflections on Motherhood and Sacrifice

It's strange at this moment, I am thinking of the song "Dear Mama" by Tupac, yet I was never in prison, never slung rocks and I certainly never put money in the mail-box or got my mom a diamond necklace, maybe Tupac was a better son then me as I never felt I did much for her, as I too was struggling just to make it at times, to keep my head above water and mom was always there, even if it meant giving me her last dime.

Bittersweet Milestones and Loss

I feel I did give her a gift in this life, which is her first and only grandchild, my daughter Mikaylah whom she loved and thankful she got to hold, kiss and spend time with her before she passed.

My mother died unexpectedly but in a way I am not surprised as her body was tired as she struggled with a poor liver and would require treatments to drain water from her legs, dying I believe to be *Cirrhosis of the liver*, but she was not a drinker, I equate her condition to having probably a fatty liver as she struggled with her weight most of her adult life with being overweight and at times obese, but I still loved her and as a child, she was mom, I didn't look at her weight, I looked at her heart, her love, although she would get frustrated with my sister and I, due to extreme pressure she was under to keep food on the table.

Although living with the Devil in his house, eating his food, using his water, it was all his and he made it known to us that we lived in his house.

This too affected my weight and my mental health as a child and I often ask myself why mom didn't get out of the verbal abuse, but deep down I understand we needed to always have a roof over our heads.

Support Through Dark Times

Mom was especially there during my darkest years in late teens when I attempted my life, putting the fear of God in her, but she and my sister and father visited me at the outpatient care facility/Mental hospital and then mom took me again.

Bittersweet Milestones and Loss

Mom's later years especially when we let her know that we were going to have a baby at her favorite restaurant Olive garden, was the same day she broke the news about her own health so it was bitter sweet and then finally the years just sped by and D day came on the exact day myself, wife, daughter and sister were enjoying a day at the Happiest Place on earth.

For some mothers hold no place in their heart because maybe mom was absent, abusive or didn't care, but my mom loved us. What I am thankful for is she gave her life to Jesus as far I know, having attending church regularly with my wife and I and she would even go by herself, so I am confident I will see her again one day.

This day is always a reminder of how short life is, how time steals from us each day and before you know it, you're old and hope that in the years passed you have got to enjoy your life, because many don't. I'll admit although I love the people in my life, I don't necessarily always enjoy my life and that is partially due to reliving what I went through in my own childhood and don't want my daughter to experience that, especially being poor.

Reflections on Life and Legacy

This day helps remind me of the impact it would have on my family if I was no longer here and yes its painful to think back and wish she was here, but I ask myself would I want her in this new world, the increase amount of pain being inflicted on this world on people.

Our society today is not immune to the pain people go through and people in our world have gone through much worse, like the Great Depression, but that doesn't mean that should experience those horrific events in history, but that it appears where our world is head. No I know my mother is in Heaven, pain free, worry free in the arms of Jesus, what better place to be.

For my life I can still look at videos of her, listen to old recordings of her singling me happy Birthday and keeping her legacy alive and her impact on my life and the people in our lives.

Preserving Her Memory

I love you mom, something I know she knew passing away at 56 years young, sadly passing young like my aunt at 46, my grandmother, material at 55, Paternal aunt at 50 years old, all died too young.

Until we meet again Mom, I love you.

Chapter 61

A Tribute to Misty McKirerman Quintana

Original title: Honoring Lost Friends: A Tribute to Misty McKirerman Quintana

July 5, 2025

Some would say you shouldn't go digging into the past, you never know what you might dig up. In my case, I have purposely dug like an archaeologist digging for only dinosaur bones, yes, I am Dr. Grant. In my case, digging through old pictures and documents of times in my life I that were both happy and incredibly sad. Remembering people is always important to me and not forgetting.

Many of those I think about are people from High school as I look through old year books, read old messages signed from friends and teachers, reminiscing my times in high school, which were the best of times and the worst of times, incredibly awkward and painful as I searched for love, but never found it. As a graduate class of 98' of Santa Fe High School, Santa Fe Springs, Go Chiefs!

This was on account of being the overweight kid, my hair slicked back and combed strangely at times, which in essence don't blame girls for finding me unattractive, I was always in the friend zone but in all truthfulness if I was ever with a girl not in the friendzone, I am afraid I would not know what to do.

Like any teenager, I had my crushes, but those girls were always unreachable, uninterested, never gave me the time of day, but I tried. I believe I was too blind to truly see the girls that attempted to pay any attention to me but that was rare. There were times so called "Friends" took advantage of my search, remembering some classmates who claimed a girl like me, but couldn't yet meet this girl, as I was provided a letter that appear legitimate and I wrote back and back , even going as far as giving my prized Turtle trinket my mother had given me, because I was big on turtles back then, never hearing back from the girl.

There was Ruth Milton, a tweaker, who I would spend a lot of time with, she would smell of weed, smoke cigarettes and I one point attempt to pick up the dirty habit to hopefully win her affection, no dice. A year after high school, I professed my love for her, which ultimately ended the friendship. There was Tiffany Witham (Now Aguirre) in drama class, a small, fresh white skinned and blond who I adored, being open with her and vulnerable even earning a single kiss on the cheek from her but were just friends.

Then there was one girl, who I believe was the one who got away, that I didn't pay any attention too, merely for the stupid fact that this girl was what I considered full figured or fat, but really, she was not but I was too blinded by meeting a thin blonde, yes, I know crazy.

Here name was Misty McKirerman but at the time didn't know her last name until I looked her up. Misty from what I remember was a strawberry blonde but now I see she was a red head. White and I believe she had green or blue eyes, a real beauty now that I think of it. She would always say high to me, talk to me and we were even going to go to Prom or Winter Formal together, but stupid me changed my mind to go with a girl that had no interest in me named Andrea.

I remember Andrea on our drive to the prom and how we were just talking in the car and one classmate said something like "Tonight is going to be a lucky night" and Andrea looked at me and said, "Not for you". Prom was not fun in my opinion, but it was like most teens a rite of passage but made the best of it. Not sure if Misty went with someone else as she was a sophomore or Junior at the time. She in Color guard at the time, but could have been band, but I was always around her because my sister was in Color guard, and I would go to all the meets.

Life went on after high school, I graduated and didn't see her much after that, but years later regretted how I treated her. Like anyone else she moved on too finding love with a gentleman named Leroy Quintana, which I never knew or met, but I am sure he is a good fellow.

Sadly, years later in 2005, a old classmate told her she had passed away, and had a child who I found his name to be Ethan. The story goes that she slipped in the shower and hit her head, causing her death.

The other reason I went searching is because of her in my mind but because of my strange interesting in reading obituaries , here is hers : Misty Quintana Obituary (2005) - Whittier, CA - Whittier Daily News.

Passing on March 23rd, 2005, who went home to be with Lord, at only 23 years old. In hope that she was a Christian and believer, in that if so I will see her again one and we can reconnect, but I doubt she would remember being, but you never know. Her son would be around 23 years old now.

Although I am not her family, or any relation to her, wanted to keep her memory alive as being very kind, beautiful and someone even today I remember, may she be resting in the LORD and that her son knows what a good person she was.

RIP Misty, a remembrance in how we never know when our lives will be unexpectedly cut short.

Chapter 62

Celebrating 15 Years of Marriage

Original title: Celebrating 15 Years of Marriage: Our Journey Together

October 5, 2025

Today I celebrated 15 years of marriage to my beautiful wife Delia. It's hard to imagine I have been married this long and at the same time it feels like a blink of an eye. My wife is such a hard worker, its apart of her DNA since I met her, even today as I think about her as a husband, asking myself the question have I been a good husband, a good provider, a person who has always treated her with love and respect and I'll admit like any couple there are the ups and downs of marriage, as marriage is the most difficult kind of relationship and I believe too often people give up to go about some semblance of their former lives. Looking back before I met Delia, I was beginning to find myself, beginning my recovery from my mental breakdown and then she came along, or better yet God placed her in my life. Our courtship was fast within 2 years of knowing each other we were married and another two years before our only daughter came along, blessing us, changing our lives forever.

It has not been easy, mostly due to my change in jobs and careers, uprooting our lives and moving in with my father in 2014 until 2018, living in what I consider to be a modern-day haunted house along with our daughter who was two at the time. This was a time that Delia really got to see me for who I was and not necessarily in a bad way, full disclosure my complete vulnerable self. The self that if I had showed her before marriage, I doubt we would have had any relationship at all because what women would stand by a manic-depressive man. Yes, I hid that well from her, in hopes that I would wake up and be a different man.

I did and do have optimism about being a better man, but let's face it I was broken and had been for many years and felt that Delia would rebuild me and in a way she did until today, but I am still broken. Broken to the point that I feel I have severely failed her in the life I promised her and hoped for.

For the most part even today I have struggled financially, going through my first Bankruptcy in 2016 after my failed attempt at a career change. I was able to rebuild, but not in the way I hoped, frankly I have never had two pennies long enough to rub together, family life is expensive, and the expenses never stop. I don't say that to place blame on my family, they are my family, my responsibility to care for, but I have failed them. We have not taken many vacations like many families do; we have not purchased that home we always wanted.

I have been on the hamster wheel of life, one life event after another, Marriage, child, work, teaching, school, paying bills and it goes on. In my heart even today, I believe she deserves and deserves better. I think that maybe before I met Delia, I was selfish to pursue her despite my flaws, but I was looking and searching for love and found it but can't help to think where I would be today If I hadn't pursued love, if I had just waited, would I be alive today, hard to say. I love my family, but I can't help but look back and forward and ask myself maybe I took Delia's chance to achieve a different type of happiness in marriage and children with someone who could give her all she deserves.

I do know that our 15 years together is an accomplishment and appreciate the love I experience each day from my family, yes, I am a blessed man and that is not lost on me. Here's to many more years to come of marriage, always looking to the future and what God has planned for us. Here's to the love I get to experience unconditionally from Delia.

Chapter 63

Turning 46: Embracing Life's Challenges

Original title: Turning 46: Embracing Life's Challenges and Blessings

December 1, 2025

Looking Back: Gratitude and Loss

Today marks my 46th birthday. While I have never been one for grand celebrations, this day inevitably prompts me to reflect on the years that have passed. For nearly two decades—17 birthdays—I have been fortunate to celebrate with my wife, my daughter, and my sister.

Yet, these occasions also remind me of loss. My mother passed away in 2015, and her absence is especially felt on days like this. I miss her dearly and wish my mother, in particular, could be here with me now.

Challenges of Recent Years

The last few years have brought significant challenges. Financial hardship and mental health struggles have cast long shadows over my life, particularly in 2023, 2024, and most of 2025.

Despite these difficulties, I recognize that there are still things for which I should be thankful—my life, above all. I admit that I do not always express this gratitude and that I often speak of death, which may not reflect an appreciation for the gift of life. Still, I know I have reasons to be thankful.

Self-Reflection and Regret

I need to do a better job of remembering the importance of life, especially my own. Over the years, I have sometimes lost respect for myself, looking back and feeling as if I should have achieved more by now. I often compare myself to others—especially those younger than me—who seem to have succeeded in ways I have not. Since graduating college in 2002, I have had 23 years to build a career, to become someone I could be proud of.

Yet, I feel I have not accomplished what I set out to do, despite my efforts. Perhaps I was too eager to live a good life and, in my haste, missed out on opportunities—to stay at certain jobs, to appreciate certain people, to savor the moments. In hindsight, I wish I had enjoyed life and those around me more fully.

The Meaning of Family and Connection

As time has gone on, more people—even beyond my family, like colleagues—have remembered my birthday, taking the time to wish me well and making me feel special. Still, it is family that matters most. My birth is not just my own milestone; it affects them most profoundly.

Lessons from "It's a Wonderful Life"

As the Christmas season approaches, I find myself reflecting on one of my favorite films, "It's a Wonderful Life." The story of George Bailey resonates with me, particularly the idea that every life has a unique purpose.

After George's uncle loses a large sum of money, George faces despair and contemplates ending his life.

The intervention of Clarence, his guardian angel, leads George to realize the impact his existence has had on others. A message from Graceway Baptist Church captures this sentiment: everyone is created for a distinct purpose, and every life matters deeply.

Even in times of discouragement or depression, we are reminded that we are loved—by those around us and, ultimately, by God, who gave His Son for us.

Seasonal Self-Reflection and the Weight of the World

I do not believe it is a coincidence that I was born in December, a month that marks the celebration of the Lord's birth and a season that naturally prompts me to reflect on my own life. In these times—both globally and within the United States—there is much that causes me anxiety and depression, especially when I think about the quality of my life and the choices I have made.

If I had made different decisions, perhaps my family and I would be in a better financial position now. Although I know that money is not everything, it holds great importance in our world. At this point in my life, I feel as though I have little, a situation for which I can only hold myself accountable. After all, I am responsible for creating the life I live today.

Embracing the Gift of Life

Yet, I am reminded that life is short—sometimes heartbreakingly so. Every day, people of all ages leave this world, some before they have had the chance to truly live. Despite the adversity I have faced, I am grateful for 46 years of life. As I age, I notice how close I am to the ages at which loved ones, such as my Aunt Liz (who died at 46 in 2006) and my mother (who passed away at 56 nearly ten years ago), left us. Still, I am here, continuing to fight and persevere.

Looking Forward with Hope

I am committed to making a greater effort to enjoy my remaining years, to appreciate the breath in my lungs and the health I have. Life is unpredictable, and I do not know when my time may come. For now, I choose gratitude. Happy birthday to me—here's to another year of life. Thank God!

I will also add, as a shameless plug that my Memoir "Runaway Shame" comes out December 1st, a gift to the world and myself.

I would be so honored if you make a purchase at most online retailers.

A MEMOIR
Runaway Shame
Joseph Gutierrez

Part VI – Career

Chapter 64

Happy 1st Work-Anniversary!

September 8, 2024

Today marks my 1 year anniversary with my current company, unbelievable how fast a year goes.

Prior to starting at my current company, I had come off months of career uncertainty, a lay off, a resignation and personal failures and burnt bridges in my job search.

This company, which is well known international company with over 50,000 employees, a juggernaut that has been around for 75 years. Never imagining I would get in as I had tried over 7 years to get my foot in the door.

I give the glory to GOD for opening this door, but by September 2023, I was broken from the past year. My confidence was shot, my mind was in torment, unable to sleep and in all honestly I was thinking of a way out of life.

From meeting my manager Michael, whom I had met a over a year prior in another interview. Michael who is warm, kind, good attitude and overall a great man. I guess I liked Mike because in my eyes he reminds alot of a better verison of myself yet younger who is about 37 years old and has been the company for about 15 years. I can not forget the other person, a director named Emy, who I too found incredibly kind, professional just incredible, but she left the company in November 23'.

Since September I have attempted to grow, learn a complex system, manage projects in a new way and learn to work with new incredible people.

From my first day, everyone has been welcome, encouraging, showing me kindness, respect and complete professionalism. Although I have worked for a few companies , no one has ever treated me like this. I will admit that may be hard to believe, I am most employers have been professional, but not every company showed they cared, not every company valued me.

This year has been filled with incredible challenges, but challenges that have progressively gotten more difficult, giving me comfort to make mistakes and learn along the away.

I continue to learn each day and have even begun seeing clients of my own now, but I am never alone as the support I need is always there.

What has also been great is the kind of people I work with from those who just started with the company to many who have been there 10,15,25,40 years amazing.

I look forward to the future of being there, but like any job there are cons, like the pay in a way is lower than what I was making before I was laid off and way less than the position I resigned from which was SCE, or shall I say forced to leave.

Most amazingly recently due exceeding departmental goals our team was gifted with a day at Disneyland, which was amazing.

Part VII – Personal Faith

Chapter 65

Palm Sunday, The Kings Arrival

Original title: Palm Sunday, The Kings Arrival That Changed The World

March 24, 2024

As a Christian, Easter is so incredibly special in a believer's life and although we are not to Easter just yet, Palm Sunday as Jesus Christ enters Jerusalem. The name Palm originates as branches waved by the crowd to greet and honor Jesus as he entered the city. This marks the holy week, which is shared across the world in western Christianity.

Taking place six days before Passover according to the book of John. Fulfilling prophecy from Zechariah 9:9, "The coming of Zion's King – See, your king comes to you, righteous and victorious, lowly and riding on a donkey, on a colt, the of foal of a donkey".

According to the Gospels, Jesus Christ rode on a donkey into Jerusalem, and celebrating people there laid down their cloaks and small branches of trees in front of him, singing part of Psalm 118: 25-26 – Blessed is he who comes in the name of the lord. We bless you from the house of the lord. The people taking out the branches of palm trees and went out to meet him, crying out, "Hosanna! Blessed is he who comes in the name of the lord, even the king of Israel!

What if find interesting is the donkey is seen as an animal of peace, unlike the horse is seen as a symbol of war. Arriving and entering as the prince of peace.

Jesus who I can only imagine was ready, but as human and God, was he afraid of what was to come, a excoriating death. I don't think any of us can fathom dying for the sins of the world, yet alone die for people we know, only Jesus could do this.

Heart breaking that today, Jesus's name is spoke in vain, with hate, with anger despite what he did for all of us, taking our sins upon him. Jesus loves the sinner no matter what and even those who do not believe in him, he still loves him and her.

This Palm Sunday, I must remember this, we must remember that there is a GOD who loves us so much, who thinks about us each day and who died for all of us.

Have a blessed Holy week!

Chapter 66

Holy Week is Here-Christ Has Risen!

March 27, 2024

Easter is a special time for me and my family, but sadly we often get busy with life, realizing that the most impactful and historical event as a Christian happened, Christ was crucified and rose again, taking up our sins for mankind. Easter although is Americanized to reflect spring, bunnies, chocolate, egg hunts is anything but a happy event, but a day Jesus gave his life for all of us on a Cross.

Unable to fathom that Jesus was born to die. Imagine having a child whose sole purpose was only to die, as a parent that is incredible hard to imagine.

Although I could never understand, as a Parent I understand that I would be willing to die for my daughter, my wife if it meant they would get something in return that would change their life for the better.

Christ Died for You and Me

Christ died so that you and I could be freed from sin, although as humans we are sinful. Laying the way for us to go to heaven, live eternally but we MUST give our lives and hearts to Jesus, which even today many are unwilling to do despite what Christ did for us.

Truly Jesus is the Way, Truth and the Life (John 14) as he has given Christians a home, when we live this earthly plane, heaven or hell are the choices, but those who reject Christ choose hell.

Hell or Heaven Awaits

Some would say, what kind of GOD send people to hell and in all trust Jesus does send people to hell, we send ourselves because we are given a choice to believe, often for many in the U.S. we are given the gospel in so many different ways, it is practically everywhere, online, on television, on the radio, in email as there really is no excuse for not knowing who Jesus is.

There are countries who do not allow the Gospel in any form, making it illegal but God and God's people find a way with underground ministries, churches, and gatherings but there are other places that it appears the gospel can not reach, but God is makes it possible and it doesn't want anything to go to Hell.

Christ died an excoriating death, beaten, whipped, hung on the cross treated worse than a common criminal, a common criminal was probably treated better in those times and even today.

Christ knew this was the toll he would have to pay for our salvation and although I can not imagine how painful it was. Having watched the passion of the Christ which I find very painful to watch seeing Christ's flesh literally ripped off, eventually no longer looking like a man.

I think about **Isaiah 53: 17-12:**

7 He was beaten, he was tortured, but didn't say a word, like a lamb taken to a be slaughtered and like a sheep sheered, he took it all in silence.

8 Justice miscarried, and he was led off – and did anyone really know what was happening? He died without a thought for his own welfare, beaten bloody for the sins of the people.

9 They buried him with the wicked, threw him in a grave with a rich man, even thought he'd never hurt a soul or said one word that wasn't true.

10 Still it's what God had in mind all along, to crush him with pain. The plan was that he given himself as an offering for sin so that he sees life come from it – life, life, and more life. And God's plan will deeply prosper through him.

No one can imagine the pain he suffered purposely, dying the most humiliating way on the cross, spit at, mocked. Today in a way is no different as people mock, laugh, curse God for their own troubles and some spread hate in the name of Jesus.

We all hurt God in our sin today, but when we give our Heart to Jesus we are forgiven, given salvation.

I know Where I'm going

I know in my heart, when I die, whether a natural death or by my own hand, that I will go to heaven. I know the last part may see controversial because one may think, well if I die by my own hand I give up my right, my salvation and should go to Hell, but I believe God doesn't strip me of my salvation because he knows I love him and I do everything in power to live a life of goodness and devotion to him, but I am still a severely flawed human, broken, but he forgives me and I am his child.

Christ made it possible to no longer fear death, as he said I have a place in heaven, filled with many mansions and I know one of those mansions he had set aside for me in paradise along with those whom I love and have passed like my mother, grandparents, loved ones, I will see them again one.

This easter, lets spread love and Joy, and yes, I know it's difficult to not make Easter about the easter bunny, eggs, springs, candy and chocolates because frankly Children especially may not fully understand what the true meaning of easter is, but why take their joy away to easter and the love that should be shared.

Personally I am guilty of buying my daughter easter baskets, chocolates eggs and candy, showering her with love and although she is 11, I share the meaning of easter and what Christ did for us, but I always want her to remember this time in her life as a time of happiness, because we should all be Happy we have a home in heaven due to Jesus paying the price for our sin.

Have a blessed Easter and **Resurrection Sunday**!

The Angel said to the women, "Do not be afraid, for I know, that you are looking for Jesus, who was crucified. He is not here; he has risen, just as he said. Come and see the place where he lay.

Matthew 28:5

Chapter 67

Why Jesus, Not Gifts, Should Define Our Holidays

December 22, 2024

What is truly important in this time of year, the season of giving, a season of joy and for myself, the reason for the season JESUS!

All of look at this time of year differently, some absolutely hate this time of year over the sear reason that it's a time of being forced to give and you may say no one forces anyone but truly people feel forced to give out of what they do not have in the form of gifts and when they can not give or will not give they are called scrooge.

I'll admit this time of year is difficult for many who struggle to keep up with giving, often having family members, friends, co-workers and also those we do not know like your postman or women, the homeless, random strangers. I personally find that my words often have meaning when I give anyone anything so if sI give a small token to others I write a personalized card which most appreciate.

I have always celebrated the traditional Christmas as you can say, the tree, presents, Food, cookies sprinkled in with some kindness and love. But as the years go on my feelings for Christmas in general have changed as I no longer see the importance of gifts but know I will never skate by NOT giving especially to my daughter who is only ten and my wife. My father, sister and other family members could care less if they get anything from me.

What I see when I go out today, is pure unadulterated consumerism people spend, spend, and spend on gifts that will go unappreciated, unused and wasted.

I often think of my favorite holiday films, "The Grinch who stole Christmas" with Jim Carrey having fond memories of watching this in the theater with a co-worker and friend at the Irvine Spectrum AMC. Why is that memory in a way so clear is because it's a time when I was at my most free, going to college, with no responsibilities and I was the young age of twenty.

But back to my story, I like the message and how the Grinch tries to teach the WHO's all of the waste they throw in the garbage, and he is the one who gets it. I can understand why, as if you have watched the film, he literally gets all of WHO Villes trash gifts. Cindy Lou, Who is actually the one who, helps open the heart of Grinch and the people of Whoville.

Sadly we here in the United States and parts of the world fail to see the importance of Jesus, Love , Kindness and that Gifts are not what's important, but we are so programmed in our world to equate this time of year as gift giving and who can blame us because the story of Christmas and Saint Nicolas who was an actual person would take his wealth and literally give it to the needy.

I get angry going to shopping centers, malls and just going out in public during these times because people are at their worst, unkind, pushy, manipulative, rude, hateful and the list goes on. Yes I know I can shop online and avoid the stores but that is beside the point because its more about how people act during this time of year truly showing their true character, which is scary.

I'd like to think we are living in kind world, country but truly we do not. People are tired, fed up and living paycheck to paycheck and this time of year pushes people over the edge and not just for financial reasons, but the way people are treated and how we treat our fellow man, women and child. WHY I ask must we treat each other in this way, because gain we have been programmed to be greedy, take advantage of people, get what is ours.

I am truly tired of how we treat people , what is it going to take because we ALL treat everyone with more kindness and respect. Do we need a national disaster, do we need a war, do we need more hardship like a full blown depression before we wake up, I hope not but feel we are ripe for that. Only GOD knows what the future holds, but feel we are ripe for a full blown dictatorship and full authoritative state and then it may be too late. Will we not learn from history on the path we are on about focusing on things that are not important.

This time of year, love more, treat others with kindness, put aside the importance of expensive gifts for 1 time in year. Instead give your time, bake something, embrace people with your words of kindness and what they mean to you.

I am sorry to say during this time of year I too have gotten wrapped up in getting the perfect gift, charging it up on my credit cards, buy, buy, spend, spend only to discover it meant nothing but what I bought would go unused, regift, trashed and for what. Why not spend quality time together this time of year and truly appreciate what you have in this life.

Truly remembering the reason for this season!

VIII- Just Thoughts

Chapter 68

The Difference Two years Makes

Original title: Self Reflection: The Difference Two years Makes, Trying to be Thankful in 2024

November 30, 2024

All the difference two years make, some of us reflect on the last year and I will surely do that in December, but for now, I look back at the last two years at a time when I can remember myself being the happiest and at peace, life was good. Not saying life is not good night now, but it has been rough, especially since last year.

Like many I look at pictures and am reminded by damn google of two years from today, five years from today, ten years from today. Pinpoints in time as I immediately think about what my life was like at that point.

Two years ago, I was at my healthiest weight, clothes fit me perfectly, my mental health, the finances were all in shape and I was ready for holidays, like Thanksgiving. Little did I know what was coming in the following year and after that. For many, some recover quickly and able to continue to momentum but not me, when I am hit hard, I am thinking how one can come down so quickly, but not everyone has a fall, but many do, so my situation is not unique as many go through far worse than what I bitch about.

I look back and get that you shouldn't, but plead with God to put me back in that place of peace in my life, not the time I am in now, where I struggle mentally, fight my inner demons as they go to battle over my thoughts and heart as I fight with the thought of just ending it all, but know I will not. For some reason I brings a smile to my face to know I have life insurance, so my family will be financially secure if something was to happen to me, whether by the hand of God or by my hand. Yes I am aware that it's wrong to think about it, but I am at a breaking point, trying to keep it together financially, trying to make sure the lights stay on, that we have a roof over our head and that the family has everything we need to be okay.

For now I should be okay, but the holidays are difficult, financially although for the most part we get through it and the family, although they doesn't get exorbitant gifts, modest gifts, it still feels as a father I have failed, as a husband, I have failed and they deserve so much better and I have vowed to give them better, even if that means I am not no longer in existence, because in my MIND, money will give them a better life, as in life insurance, which is what its there for. For those who say, well life insurance doesn't cover suicides, but in fact it does and my policies do just as long as I don't do anything within two years of taking out a policy, called appropriately the suicide clause. After two years is up, the insurance company is required to pay out. You see, the clause is primarily in place for those who used to take out policies and the following month kissed the world goodbye, not me, as two years is like a blink of a eye, as I plan.

Some of you may be thinking this is not being very thankful and that I should be more grateful for my life. I am grateful for my life indeed, but I wanted to give my family the best life, again in my mind feel they can have a wonderful life without me. Yes, I am aware that it would be difficult over my loss but in time they would eventually see I did what I did for the best and they were in a better place.

I know many may not think like I do, these thoughts stick in my cranium and stay there, maybe in 2025 I should seek some help, as I do always hope for the best ,that things will turn a corner and then in two years from now, I will look back and be thankful that didn't take life ending steps, but well aware once I take the final leap, that will be it and it all honestly it wont be leap, it will be the tug of a rope around my neck or the smell of carbon monoxide from the engine of a car, as I go into a deep, deep sleep. No, I wouldn't be jumping off some ten-story building as I go splat on the sidewalk, or a gunshot wound as I have no gun and too afraid of blood to cut myself, I have my methods and speaking from experience know what the tug of the rope around my neck feels like.

For now, I will live in memory lane as I attempted to remember the good times, the years past when Thanksgiving was the time, I said thank you for having peace in my life and when life was good.

God never promises times to be perfect and I know that. Because God can change the times, our life whenever he chooses and it's all for his own reasons.

I do pray everyone had a great Thanksgiving and have a better perspective than I do during this time. God Bless all!

Chapter 69

One year Ago Today Dread Came Knocking

Original title: One year Ago Today Dread Came Knocking: Job loss, Despair and Regret

February 28, 2024

February 28th, 2023, will be an unforgettable day, as I woke up early Tuesday morning for a client meeting, checking my phone first thing at 6:30 A.M only to see my teams apps was not working, which I found to be strange, attempting to login in again, unable to.

Life Changing Email

Feeling the need to check my e-mail, seeing a dreaded e-mail from the company I had been with for almost three years with the words Layoff, Restructuring, Elimination, 9% and apologies, Human resources. I was done, cut, I was not jobless leaving me in shock, another layoff, this being the 3rd one since 2018.

I guess in a way I expected it with all the tech layoffs that were taking place in that year and the year before. My wife and daughter still sleeping as I work up my wife telling her the news, as I contemplated if I should wake her and tell her, but I needed her kind words, to know that everything was going to be okay, but I was shaken. Reading the Email, there was a time and link to a zoom meeting at 9:40 am with HR and my manager. I was able to finally get into my work computer, because at first, I was unable to, again strange. Getting in and seeing an e-mail from the C.E.O, this e-mail.

The news spread in my work e-mail as colleagues within our team chat were saying goodbye and thanking each other for the support. One of my co-workers reaching out to me directly, saying goodbye, but shocked to hear I was one of those let go as he was upset that I was let go.

I did also say my goodbyes as my computer access was going to be shut down in a few hours. Fear struck across the team's chat as many who were not laid off were scared of what was to come for them. I said my goodbyes, took down some contact information and gave them mine and logged off for good.

My Denial

At first, I was in denial about my job loss, thinking how this could happen, why, what did I do to deserve this, what does this seem to always happen to me, why is it I can not have the stability in my work most tend to have, what am I so worthless.

One year Ago Today Dread Came Knocking: Job loss, Despair and Regret.

February 28th, 2023, will be an unforgettable day, as I woke up early Tuesday morning for a client meeting, checking my phone first thing at 6:30 A.M only to see my teams apps was not working, which I found to be strange, attempting to login in again, unable to.

Life Changing Email

Feeling the need to check my e-mail, seeing a dreaded e-mail from the company I had been with for almost three years with the words Layoff, Restructuring, Elimination, 9% and apologies, Human resources. I was done, cut, I was not jobless leaving me in shock, another layoff, this being the 3rd one since 2018.

I guess in a way I expected it with all the tech layoffs that were taking place in that year and the year before. My wife and daughter still sleeping as I work up my wife telling her the news, as I contemplated if I should wake her and tell her, but I needed her kind words, to know that everything was going to be okay, but I was shaken. Reading the Email, there was a time and link to a zoom meeting at 9:40 am with HR and my manager. I was able to finally get into my work computer, because at first, I was unable to, again strange. Getting in and seeing an e-mail from the C.E.O, this e-mail.

The news spread in my work e-mail as colleagues within our team chat were saying goodbye and thanking each other for the support. One of my co-workers reaching out to me directly, saying goodbye, but shocked to hear I was one of those let go as he was upset that I was let go.

I did also say my goodbyes as my computer access was going to be shut down in a few hours. Fear struck across the team's chat as many who were not laid off were scared of what was to come for them. I said my goodbyes, took down some contact information and gave them mine and logged off for good.

My Denial

At first, I was in denial about my job loss, thinking how this could happen, why, what did I do to deserve this, what does this seem to always happen to me, why is it I can not have the stability in my work most tend to have, what am I so worthless.

I will say that although I was surprised, I was also looking for a change, but not like this as who wants to be forced to job search as the previous year, I was in the job search, but nothing came of it. What did help was the severance, which I will say was okay, enough to last a few months but knew that money went fast especially with rent, bills, food, car payment so I know it wouldn't last long. Going into the end of the month and into March, I had no idea what the year was going to turn out to be giving myself a short break of two weeks to have some time to myself, plus I had a surgical procedure on March 20th.

I went about my life for the time being, slowly seeing what the job market looked like on LinkedIn and other sites and there appeared to be jobs, but little did I know in how bad the job market was. If I was single with no family or real responsibilities, I would have been ok, but add a wife and daughter and the pressure is on to hurry up.

Finding My Next Work Home

Was I concerned at that point, not confident I should find something, but I did begin slowly to apply knowing I probably won't hear back for a few weeks. Applying with a few trusty companies I had a applied with in the pasted, one being the company I am at now.

A couple of weeks went by getting a couple call backs and interviews, but nothing came of it. A short time after I got a manager reaching out to me through LinkedIn stating they may be interested seeing that I was recently laid off. It happened to have been with a company I was aware of. Thinking it would be great to get hired so quickly but in the end, I end up interviewing with two sets of interviewers, but nothing came of it.

I continued to apply and again I began to get some nibbles towards the end of March, two companies in fact and good ones. One of them, for a credit union and another for Southern California Edison. Both exciting opportunities and both interviews going well. In a matter of weeks I had a few other interviews, but two companies in the running, coming to the week of April 20th, getting two job offers with good pay increases.

Wrong Choices and Regrets

This is where things for me started to turn as I told both companies, I wanted those jobs but wouldn't be starting for a few weeks due to background, giving me time to decide. I should have just told one of the companies NO and moved on but deep down I was fearful of one of the roles falling through, so I held on to them.

Indecision Destroyed Me

I could not decide, deep down I wanted the Edison position, but it was so different than my previous roles, where the Credit Union was like the type of work I was doing previously. Deep down I shouldn't have been concerned, after all as a man of faith, I should have had more faith in GOD that he provided both roles for me and was giving me a choice. It's not that I didn't trust the Lord, it was I didn't trust myself and frankly didn't know truly what role I wanted. My mental state was not in a good place, having lost another role in a short time having had to look for a job 3 years prior.

I did decide to accept the Edison role, but I did end up burning a bridge with the credit union as I kept going back and forth on accepting and declining the role and as expected they just got tired and declined the role to me.

I attempted to move forward, be happy I had a job lined up and one with a company that I had been trying to work for and for years at that.

New Job, but not what I expected

Starting May 15th, 2023, as a Senior Support Project Specialist, working in a hybrid role in Pomona, California, 3 days at home, 2 in the office, compared to being fully remote previously. I thanked GOD for the opportunity and prayed the new role would bring me prosperity for years to come. I did have this gut feeling that I should have stuck with the credit union, which also happened to be a Christian Credit union, an organization that aligned with my beliefs. Attempting to not overthink and be happy, starting my new role.

Gut Feelings I Ignored

The first day as if I walked on the vast building meeting great people, I still had this gut feeling as if I made a mistake. Like any new job, its new and stressful as I take on a new journey in a new environment. Overall, everyone seemed great, nice and professional. My new manager Stephen and Supervisor Tabitha were great and then there was no colleague Blanca, a twenty-year employee project manager.

My gut feeling was not in fact the company itself but her for some reason, having interviewed with her twice virtually, she seemed nice, professional, someone I could work with but meeting her in person there was something about her. Attempting to put those feelings aside, going through origination, preparing for training.

I began to shadow an employee who was incredibly nice, professional and patient with me, with me for three weeks and then I would be left on my own with the Project manager Balana. Three weeks came and went fast and before I know it was her right hand man so to speak, hitting meetings, reviewing agendas, getting caught up to speed on the job.

My New Hell Began

There was really no formal training, It was on me to learn the job and ask for help from those around me, which I did. It seemed soon that she begins to disagree, criticize how I was attempting to do my job, speaking directly with my manager who would then let me know, never directly telling me. The structure of my role is that she did not have the same manager I did and add to that I was considered a contractor, not an employee.

From there it went down hill as she appeared to only get worse and I never really confronted her about attitude towards me or my manager as I thought she will loosen up when I learned my role fully, but no This was who she was a hardnosed, Micromanaging Latin women. Some may thing what does her being Latin have to do with anything. Being a Mexican Immigrant, having told me she crossed the border early in her life, having fought to get to her position and that was why she was so tough, having a chip on her shoulder and an accent.

Again, some may say well what is wrong with that, nothing really but I grew to had a distaste for her, her attitude, the way she acted like I was less than and in my eyes this women forgot where she came from. Come to find out she treat most people like this, especially the people before me.

The Final Straw

The final straw was on July 8th, when my point of contact, the contracting company rep Ari advised me he had spoken to the client Edison and was advised they wanted to place me on a PIP plan (Performance Improvement Plan), a type of probation for 60 days.

I would be required to sign off on the probation to basically keep my job, which I found offensive, add to that I had NEVER been on a PIP plan before, so I stood my ground and didn't wish to sign. The company unwilling to work with me, forfeiting my position. This threw me into a tales pin of despair, as I had a family to care for, bills, as I second guessed my decision but it was too late.

My Year Of No Peace

I would say from the time of unemployment throughout that time, I was unable to sleep, rest, feel peace and my mental state was getting worse. Add to that, I had several attempts to get the job at the credit union back, reaching out to them directly but those e-mails were ignored.

It was around June, I had decided to reach out to my current company ADP, who back in April wanted to interview me, but had declined due to getting a job offer already. It was at this time, the recruiter had finally reached out to me, from when I reached out in June.

They were still interested and wanted me to interview, and I agreed having my interview on July 12th which obliviously went great, than another interview two weeks later, then finally three weeks later I got offered the Job and one cane say the rest is history having been here at ADP since September 5th, 2023.

Onward and Upward

I look forward to the future here as everyone here as been nothing but kind, professional and not an ounce of that gut feeling I got at Edison. Financially and mentally, it will be hard to recover but I am try each day but feel I will not fully be better until later this year.

2023 will be a year I will never forget, it has scared me for a long time and many will say just move on, forget about that time and I am trying to, but I am sorry to say those mistake I made prevent me from forgetting as what really I think about is the money lost from those two earlier positions and although I am doing ok now, I did take a pay cut in my role, but there are better opportunities here and better people in my opinion. I look forward to hopefully being here many years, but only GOD knows what his plans are for my time here.

Never Give Up!

For those who have had similar experiences in being laid off, fires, leaving jobs than you can relate. Finding a good fit is never easy but its position. Mistakes are going to happen but we must overcome those mistakes and remember life is often messy, but we have the ability to correct most mistakes and attempt to live happy, prosperous lives.

Here's to a better year!

Chapter 70

Life, Death, and Turning 45

Original title: Life, Death, and Turning 45: A Moment of Reflection

December 2, 2024

Today is my 45th birthday, a mini milestone to the BIG 5-0, which is daunting in a way and although we all get older, which is normal it only brings to focus my morality and what I have truly done in this life. I am not rich, nor do I have a fancy job title or am I am man of importance, even to the point of leading people in my work, I am a nobody. For many some would say who cares if you are no a nobody, there are lots of nobodies in this world and they are pretty content being nobody and maybe I should be. Except for most of my adult life where I can't help but look back and think of the failures in my life, despite me working towards success, never reaching there. Although anything can happen in this life, I doubt very much that could happen, as I look around much younger colleagues are recognized and promoted, I guess I am past my prime. I would love to be one of those glasses half full kind of people, I am not. The reality is as I grow older, I grow less relevant like many people, I know I am no different.

It's sad that I can not enjoy today, although I have my wife and daughter in my life, I should look at what I do have instead of what I don't have. But what I don't have in this life affects what I do have like my wife and daughter.

Today is no celebration but it forces me to self-reflect again and again on my life and when I when it will be my time to leave this earthly plane. Life and death got together, just like birth and death, they are both inevitable. I truly do not believe I will live to see my 46th birthday, which is unfortunate because of what has happened in my life and what continues to bring me deeper and deeper into desolation, something no one can help.

Birthdays should be a time to be thankful for one's life and the breath we breathe each day and I guess one can say it's a matter of perspective and that my perspective is poor, so change it. I can not because my belief is so now ingrained in how I see myself, I feel its almost impossible.

I pray I am wrong with this being my last birthday, but each day, week I plan for that moment, to leave my wife and daughter in a better place. Although I know it will be difficult for them and that my loss to their life with forever felt, they will recover, and they will be able to enjoy this life like I intended. I pray that I will have joy again, have a smile again, but sadly a lot of that depends not just on me, but the people around me and even those people who have indirect effect over their support. For instance, I have often email my church for prayers and guidance, only to be told I need to come and they can pray for me then, but offer no words of wisdom , of kindness despite me being very clear that I am not in a good place, but sure I will come instead of the pastor offering me some words of kindness to get me through the day, only confirming I am a no body in fact. I get GOD says I am someone, I am important to him, but where is he at times. That is not to put down God, I know God is silent at times, but this is not the time I need him to be silent.

I get God wants me to get on my knees and pray and I do, and he does answer, but for what I am struggling with, personal and financial loss at this time in my life, I am broken on this 45th birthday and there is not a damn thing anyone can do and will do to be there, I am at a loss.

Afterword

It is my hope that if read my volume three blogs, you are not bored, but find my words expressive, touching your heart and soul, as it is my goal that my readers feel connected to me. I know this volume is certainly different then volume one and two, as you can see I almost have become politicized, having have written about the state of our country and specifically our current president, which was not my intention, but goes to show how affected I was and am today to what is going on today in our country and the world, it brings me great anxiety. I am working harder not to write about our rage of political issues, because it can certainly turn people off about me and who I am, forcing readers to turn away, thinking I am so nut who has nothing else to write about. I have lots to write about, I have lots of emotions and feelings to express and I hope you see that in my writing, especially around mental health.

I tend to live in the past a little too much at times, something else I am working on each day and living in the present as life as new troubles each day, it helps not to too to much in the past as it's the past.

I will say if I maintain my future volumes, my next volume will come out in 2028 with volume 4, which I hope to continue to offer readers, as you see my growth and change, which if you ready volume 1 and 2, I do feel you see the change in me and how I have grown over the years.

I am very honored for those who read my blogs and my books and hope you find them enjoyable and worth your time. Continue to keep an eye out for future work, as I am regularly putting out novels adding to my repertoire of work. Thank you again for your patronage and support, I couldn't do this without you.

Works

Short Stories

- Gutierrez, Joseph., **Short Stories from a Child's Mind – Animal Friends Edition**, Pub. May 12th, 2024, ISBN: 9798869320803, 68 pgs.
- Gutierrez, Joseph., **Short Stories from a Child's Mind – Swashbuckler & Gunslinger Edition**, Pub. June 18th, 2024, ISBN: 9798869332608, 84 pgs.
- Gutierrez, Joseph., **Short Stories from a Child's Mind – The Monster's Edition**, Pub. July 8th , 2024, ISBN: 9798869341525, 40 pgs.
- Gutierrez, Joseph., **Short Stories from a Child's Mind – A Collection**, Pub. Aug 30th, 2025, ISBN: 9798348540555, 180 pgs.
- Meyer, Joe R., **Triggered: Book of Blogs-Volume 1**, Pub. July 18, 2025, ISBN: 9798348575472, 414 pgs.
- Meyer, Joe R., **Unhinged: Book of Blogs-Volume 2**, Pub. November 14, 2025, ISBN: 9798349214493, 454 pgs.

Non-Fiction

- Gutierrez, Joseph., **Folklore: History, Short Stories of Yaqui and Tohono O'odham Indigenous People**, 9798349526671, 450 pgs.
- Gutierrez, Joseph., **The Forgotten Son-Chapter 2**, Pub. Oct 31st, 2025: 9798348532901, 282 Pgs.
- Gutierrez, Joseph., **The Forgotten Son-Chapter 1**, Pub. June 15th, 2025: 9798348523930, 204 Pgs.
- Gutierrez, Joseph., **The Forgotten Son-Chapter 3**, Pub. Feb 7, 2026: 9798348545369, 302 Pgs.
- Gutierrez, Joseph., **The Forgotten Son**, Pub. February 7th, 2025: 9798348211059, 840 Pgs.
- Meyer, Joe R., **Freaks, Life in The Circus from Yesterday to Today**, Pub. September 23, 2025, ISBN: 9798349214844, 352 pgs.
- Gutierrez, Joseph., **Runaway, Shame: A Memoir**, Pub. Dec 1, 2025: 9798348578039, 256 Pgs.

Novels

- Meyer, Joe R., **A Shot in The Dark**, Pub, ISBN: 9798349526619, 574 pgs.
- Meyer, Joe R., **Alien-Squatch Wars**, Pub June 30, 2026, ISBN: 9798349587344, 160 pgs.
- Meyer, Joe R., **Whispers**, Pub, April 8, 2026, ISBN: 9798349526640, 296 pgs.
- Meyer, Joe R., **The Pox**, Pub. June 18, 2023, ISBN: 9781088235973, **First Edition (Out of Print)**
- Meyer, Joe R., **The Pox**, Pub. January 18th, 2025, **Second Edition**, ISBN: 9798330560424, 420 pgs.
- Meyer, Joe R., **The Menagerie Locket**, Pub. March 17th, 2024, ISBN: 9798869186348, 254 pgs.
- Meyer, Joe R., **Pounds of Flesh**, Pub. October 2nd, 2024, ISBN: 9798330371617, 246 pgs.
- Meyer, Joe R., **Doll Parts**, Pub. September 7th, 2025, ISBN: 9798348559441, 294 pgs.

www.ingramcontent.com/pod-product-compliance
Lightning Source LLC
LaVergne TN
LVHW052223200926
848481LV00001B/199
* 9 7 9 8 3 4 8 4 8 2 8 6 2 *